YOGA
For Men Only

FRANK R. YOUNG, D.C.

PARKER PUBLISHING COMPANY, Inc.
West Nyack, N. Y.

Books by Frank Rudolph Young

Cyclomancy: The Secret of Psychic Power Control
The Laws of Mental Domination
Psychastra: the Key to Secret ESP+ Control
The Secrets of Personal Psychic Power

LIBRARY OF CONGRESS
CATALOG CARD NUMBER: 73-77626

PRINTED IN THE UNITED STATES OF AMERICA
13-972398-6 B&P

What This Book Can Do for You

The well-guarded Yoga secrets revealed for the first time in this book have been used by the Yogis for thousands of years to improve every part of their bodies, from head to foot, and have transformed them into vastly superior men physically and mentally.

You can do the same thing for yourself. Without the modern scientific knowledge of the human body to guide them, though, the Yogis did it the "hard" way, the long way, the torture way. You, of course, cannot expect to achieve the remarkable transformations which they did, in just seconds a day. But you *can* achieve in that time *all you need* to drastically change your whole life, physically, socially and in business, and attain successes which might now seem impossible to you.

Some of the wonderful Yoga transformations that can be yours!

Using the well-guarded Yoga secrets revealed for the first time in this book, you can scientifically bring about *all you need* of those transformations in yourself very quickly. For example, you can acquire:

1. A young, or much younger looking, face—or a face looking as much as 20 to 30 years younger than you are in calendar years.

2. A long, or much longer life—perhaps up to 50 years longer than you might live otherwise. Living 100 years is nothing exceptional for a Yogi; many Yogis are reputed to have reached 150, 200 years or more.

3. A trim waist. No matter how big your waist is now, with the simple, *strainless* movements of *Yogametrics* you can pare it down to that of youthfulness and in surprisingly short time.

4. Supple hard muscles. No matter how flabby your muscles

are, you can tone them up rapidly and *strainlessly* with *Yogametrics* and feel like a young athlete.

5. Sex power.   With Yoga secrets, you can charge your aging sex glands with renewed potency.

6. Strong back and fresh brain.   When you are weary during, or at the end of, the day, you can tone up your back and your brain in a few seconds, *right while you are at your desk*, bench, or any place.

7. Faster success.   Any time you confront, at work or in your career, someone who surpasses you or makes you feel inferior to him, you can regain your confidence and vanquish him, or gain his full respect instantly, by contracting invisibly and unsuspectedly a specific muscle-combine in just seconds.

8. Manly sex appeal at any age.   When the woman you want ignores you, and you feel that you have no chance with her, you can hold her keen interest in you at once, with a Yoga secret.

9. Self-defense.   When cornered by a bully who can demolish you with a blow, you can hold him at bay and scare him off promptly.

And that's just the beginning!

How you can transform your whole body physiology with Yoga secrets

You can also transform your whole body physiology with these well-guarded Yoga secrets, and combat any number of common diseases, particularly before they devitalize you and hurry old age.

The well-guarded Yoga secrets are especially perfected for:

constipation	anxiety
fatigue	fear
stomach and intestinal	subclinical diabetes
disorders	aging of the age-controlling
backaches	glands
stiff joints and muscles,	strain hernia
leading to arthritis	sacroiliac

unfavorable blood pressure	flabby muscled heart
headaches (non-pathologic)	varicose veins
bronchitis	hemorrhoids
rheumatism	vague, nagging
nervous tension	symptomless pains

The crippling Four Horsemen of the Mastabah

These well-guarded Yoga secrets, best of all, rescue you from the merciless, inescapable, Four Horsemen of the Mastabah. Your inescapable enemies are:

1. The downpull of gravity.
2. Faulty posture.
3. Weight-bearing.
4. Ground resistance.

These four insidious forces attack you relentlessly 24 hours a day, particularly when you are standing or sitting. They drag down and distort your skeletal framework . . . misshape it, so that it functions inefficiently . . . tear it down . . . and consume an alarming proportion of your natural, inborn energy in just resisting them. They weaken disastrously your natural capacities to resist disease, to look young, to live longer. They keep you *progressively subclinically ill* from the moment you are born and hasten you to an untimely grave—many years ahead of the natural lifespan of your body cells. They accomplish that directly through building up abnormally in your body the ever-threatening, death-dealing infiltration acids which are ever present in your body cells. Yoga possesses the secret for repressing these unbanishable enemy infiltrations, and thereby prolonging your health, energy, youth, sex power and lifespan.

A healer teaches you how to use Yoga for men only

My paternal ancestors (descending from long-lived Yogis in far-off India) spent nearly 100 years gathering these well-guarded Yoga secrets, and I have studied them all my life. In connection with my training as a Doctor of Chiropractic, I then sought their scientific foundations. When satisfied that I had found them, I refined the crude methods and perfected the effectiveness of these hard, long, torturing Yoga disciplines. I

discovered, moreover, from X-ray films of many who had practiced Yoga without the benefit of science, that some of their
postures and disciplines were very harsh, particularly to the neck
and back. This was due to the fact that the Yogis themselves
were not professionally trained in the sciences of anatomy, physiology, pathology, neurology or diagnosis. Consequently, I *eliminated completely* from these secrets, those which did as much
harm as good, and retained and refined only those which bring
you wonderful results safely, strainlessly and healthily. *Yoga for
Men Only*, by a Doctor of Chiropractic, is therefore a qualified,
safe, wholly beneficial, scientific practice of Yoga the easy way.
Thousands have been helped—safely—by the revealed secrets of
modern procedures pertaining to its safe practice. You can prove
these benefits for yourself by following the self-help programs in
this book in a minimum of your spare time. It can be the best
investment you can ever hope to make.

Frank Rudolph Young, D.C.

What Yoga Can Do For a Man 1

How to conquer the four horsemen of the mastabah that disease you, cripple you, age you, and kill you prematurely

The four deadly horsemen of the mastabah (the four horsemen of the early grave) are the:

1. constant downpull of gravity
2. faulty posture
3. weight-bearing
4. ground resistance

Were it not for the body traumas to which these four horsemen subject you all your life, you would conserve such a great amount of energy daily and hourly that you would be practically *immune to disease*; you would age *much more slowly*; you would look younger and live *considerably longer*. Such a state, though, is possible only in something like the "spirit state"—or in a state in which absolutely no energy is expended to remain alive—no energy even to breathe, much less to digest food, circulate blood, transmit nerve messages or commands, or get rid of body wastes. Indeed, no energy even to look, hear, touch, swallow, cough, adjust to changes of temperature, endure pain, grow hair. As a matter of fact, *not even* energy to think, harbor emotion, dream, desire, reproduce, repair tissue and the rest of the infinite number

1

of physiological activities which your body functions maintain. All your body functions, in brief, would have to come to a halt, and your tissues would have to remain lifeless but super-alive in another plane of existence.

The knowledgeable Yogi, however, *can* prolong his life to an almost unbelievable age. He can also resist or overcome disease with seemingly miraculous ease. He possesses something akin to limitless energy, both mental and physical. He can sit naked on ice in freezing weather and *perspire*. And that's a mere sampling of the astounding achievements which he can bring about with his body.

How can he do this? He can do it because, primarily, he carries, reserved within his mind and body, a great amount of energy which he regularly saves by lessening considerably the effects on himself of the body traumas of the four horsemen of the mastabah previously described.

Your first goal, then, is to minimize, as much as possible, the ceaseless drain on your body of the relentless body traumas of the four horsemen of the mastabah. Any posture which you assume, in fact, drains your energy because it compels you to overcome the constant downpull of gravity, if nothing else. Faulty posture, though, drains your energy still faster because it displaces the center of gravity of your body from its best-balanced point to a less-balanced point. Consequently, your joints are subjected to abnormal wear-and-tear every time you make a move, and their supporting muscles are thrown into abnormal spasms, in order to balance your now unbalanced body against the pull of gravity.

Your imbalanced body, besides, increases the amount of energy which your body has to waste resisting the pull of gravity, the push of weight-bearing and the jarring of the ground from below. Correct posture, therefore, conserves your body energy constantly and reduces the ceaseless drain on your body of the four horsemen of the mastabah. A long lasting youth and a long life, for that reason, are absolutely dependent upon how much you lessen daily the body traumas of gravity, faulty posture, weight-bearing and ground resistance on you.

Benefits of freeing yourself enough from the downpull of gravity alone

If you could just free yourself enough from the downpull of

gravity alone, leaving its pull on you *only strong enough* to keep you still attracted to the earth, but to subject you to the least body traumas, you could live much longer and:

Your joints would not suffer from the wear-and-tear afflictions of old age or of excessive use, such as arthritis.

You would not sprain a joint or break a bone.

You would suffer from *no* infectious diseases, because your physiological resistance would be omnipotent against all attacks of diseases.

Your body organs would require hardly any nutrition and would exist many times longer.

You would be practically tireless, regardless of effort.

And that's hardly scraping the surface of how different your life would be. BUT—since you cannot lessen the relentless downpull of gravity on you, Yoga has devised ways to *counteract* its insidious influence on your body to a gratifying degree. Wrong foods, psychological traumas, and practically every other assault against your body and mind would affect you little if you could only *save* within you the vast amount of energy you waste trying to combat the downpull of gravity every second of your life. You would *then* most closely approximate the spirit state of immortality, agelessness and healthfulness and you would require hardly any food for existence. Your mind would feel so remarkably refreshed constantly that it could think, remember and attain other mental goals with a facility which you hardly consider possible now.

The constant threat of the unsuspected, undermining, subclinical state which exists in you

Due to the merciless pounding of the four horsemen of the mastabah on your body throughout your life, you are never the person you might be were the downpull of gravity on you much less, and especially if it were only strong enough to keep you attracted to the earth. As a result, you degenerate into a battered victim of body trauma and grow steadily worse with years, even long before you experience obvious pain or exhibit diagnostic symptoms. Between the limits of normal health and outright disease, in fact, there exists a wide expanse of so-called "well enough" health states which range from your not feeling at your

very best, to your feeling on the border of being sick. Throughout that health range you are not ill enough to consult a physician. You are still in the subclinical state. Indeed, even though
you continue to be battered and grow steadily worse under the
relentless pounding of the four body traumas over the years, you
might *never* experience obvious pain or exhibit diagnostic symptoms because of it.

Within you, however, there is a steadily growing discord between your mind and body, for your battered body is unable
to drive home forcibly enough to your mind how badly it really
feels, because your mind instinctively avoids sensitizing itself to
the unpleasant by inhibiting its reaction to it. Your mind, however,
cannot inhibit indefinitely its reaction to that ceaseless flow of
messages of vague pains and general discomforts which your body
flashes to it. Thus, it tries to escape from the impasse by venting
its annoyance *outside* your body, such as by assuming unpleasant
attitudes, unexplainable hostility to others, pessimisms, groundless
fears and anxieties, hypochondria and other unaccountable be-
havior.

Physicians of no healing art have given this extensive, perplex-
ing, indefinable attitude of most "normal patients" enough study
and have depended too much upon the X-ray, the laboratory
analysis and the psychiatric test for the final word about the
seemingly insignificant complaints of the patient. They have not
added to their diagnosis, the sub-diagnosis of the unfelt, but
cumulative effect of the steady battering of the four horsemen
of the mastabah on the patient.

Yoga for Men Only has taken that step for the first time and
shows you how the Yogis prepare themselves to combat and
neutralize, as much as possible, the relentless crippling of the
horsemen of the mastabah and thereby save for themselves much
of the vast amount of energy which their bodies regularly waste
in attempting to resist them. The Yogis, for that reason, look
younger, grow powerful more easily, retain their sex potency
longer, keep their minds sharper, and live surprisingly longer.
The following case histories reveal how others, just like you,
have altered their lives in a very short time with the scientifically
perfected Yoga secrets, and how you too can do likewise, or even
much more.

How Richard acquired a dynamic aspect of personal appeal

Richard, 42 years old, was tired of being an insignificant no-body with a typical job, typical prospects, typical appearance, and of being less than extraordinary with women. Yet, there was a woman of about 24 or 25 who made his head spin. They passed each other regularly in the lunch crowd, in the lobby of the big office building where they worked. Richard watched her from the corner of his eye and sighed in despair. He felt totally out of the running. He was already graying noticeably and was developing a receding hairline, but he couldn't get that girl out of his mind. She even affected his work adversely.

Richard met me through a mutual friend. When he found himself alone with me, he confessed his dilemma.

I taught him a Yoga secret. After practicing it *only twice* he felt so differently that he could hardly believe he was the same person.

Next day, he again encountered his goddess in the crowded lobby at lunch time. To his disbelief, for the *first time ever,* her eyes lingered on his pleasantly as she passed.

After that, Richard was like a hound let loose after the fox. He spoke to the young lady, lunched with her, dated her and married her five and a half months later.

Richard was so commonplace and insignificant-looking that, no matter how little you think of yourself, you can enjoy *at least* the same success he did. You no longer need to feel that you haven't a chance with a woman, just because she is much younger than you, is pursued feverishly by far more attractive men than you, possesses a beauty of face or figure that stuns people, or is very intelligent, well educated, or belongs to a family of means. With the well-guarded Yoga secrets you thrust aside all those barriers *instantly* and force that goddess of yours to see *you* as *her* god, no matter how insignificant you look, or how unspectacular your life prospects are. Because, with your body charged with extra Spino-Volt power, and with the secret Yoga posture to give you sex appeal, you will suddenly present a new, dynamic aspect to that princess of yours that will speed up her heart beat and incite her to know you and win you for herself.

**How 53-year-old Charles built up his rundown, distorted frame
and drew admiration for himself for his "physique"**

At 53 Charles was a married man with two children already
out of college and on their own. With their added leisure, he and
his wife Edith spent several hours a day on the city beach in the
summer. As Charles watched the young muscle men roam the
beach, arresting all eyes with their clean-cut, shapely muscles,
V-shaped backs and their overall look of personal power, he felt
that life had passed him by, that he had never had time to develop his own body and look like something worth looking at
twice. Instead, he had been a lifetime work horse. He did not
regret marrying his Edith and raising his kids, but he secretly
wished now that he had done a little more for his personal self,
instead of just letting himself "go to pot." What would he give
now to look like somebody—*to look a little like those fellows!* Who
bothered to watch *him*, except to wonder that he had the courage
to wear a bathing suit in public. His whole torso was smooth and
flabby, like a woman's. He was afraid even to lift weights. He
had tried to once, and had strained himself badly. Besides, it too
much resembled hard labor. He had tried isometrics, too, but his
doctor had advised him against halting his circulation with it.

Charles confided his dreams to me, and I taught him the Yogametric secret of simple, two-second contractions of his muscles at
their right angles of pull, for fast body building. Charles was enthusiastic because it required none of the arduous straining of
weight-lifting, and none of the long-holding, painful, blood-
clotting possible dangers of isometrics.

It astonished everybody how swiftly Charles' body changed
with Yogametrics. His flabby flesh melted away day after day as
if by magic, and his "new muscles" were carving eye-catching
contours all over him. His shoulders broadened steadily, while
his "pregnant-looking belly," as his friends were wont to joke
about it, trimmed down in front and narrowed at the sides. His
flat chest, meanwhile, bulged upwards, neatly carved out, and
endowed him with a forceful, manly, but youthful look. More
and more beachgoers commented on his startling change and
stopped teasing him. The solid feeling Charles was gaining, too,

filled him with an exuberance he had not enjoyed since child-hood. Before summer ended, his development already suggested that of a young muscle man who had "taken it easy" for a few weeks and had lost some of his muscle bulk and clean muscle separation, but whose body still showed marked, concealed muscle development.

In less than one summer, with Yogametrics, and only *49 seconds* a day, Charles had built up his rundown, distorted frame and, for once in his life, drew admiration for himself when he donned his bathing suit.

How you can build up your figure at any age

You, too, can do as well as Charles, or far better, in amazingly short time, with just seconds a day, for he started out with a long list of counts against him. He was unusually short in stature, startlingly misshapen, unbelievably narrow-shouldered, indescribably flat chested, alarmingly "pot bellied," profusely varicosed in the legs, and suffered from flat feet. But he changed his whole life with certain well-guarded Yoga secrets—just 49 seconds a day.

With two-second Yogametric contractions, your muscles can also grow and get solid quickly because you contract them at their *right angles* of pull. And since you devote only 49 seconds a day to them, they don't fatigue, but are only toned up youth-fully and *flexibly* for the rest of the day. The fat covering them is worn off without exhausting you; consequently, you are steadily *improving*, rather than recuperating first *before* improving. You muscles, as a result, get harder day-after-day, and carve exciting, youthful, and elastic lines and curves all over your body. The youthful spring returns to your step and carries you along easily when you walk. Your new, flat, narrow waist arouses envy and admiration and persuades others to accept you as signifi-cantly younger than you claim to be. Young people now see you as "in" instead of as an "old goat." Even your children proudly claim you as their father. Men from 30 to 80, everywhere, will ask you how you can keep in such fine shape. Since most people, too, prefer that kind of figure to "big, ugly muscles," as they call the muscle man's, they call *your* figure the *right* figure. You are no longer a physical nonentity, but someone whom so many would like to look like.

NOTE: If you desire a big bulky, muscular physique like the huge-muscled strong man, or the big muscular, but well-proportioned physique of the Mr. America type, Yogametrics can give you one, too. In one year I myself built up with Yogametrics from an average 155 lbs. to a thickly muscular 215 lbs. after frustratingly trying for remarkable gains from weight-lifting and other methods. I had changed my diet comparatively little, too! With Yogametrics my muscles seemed to *absorb* and retain more building proteins from my regular diet and grew much faster in size and power. In order to attain such a stupendous gain, of course, you have to do your Yogametric movements at least one hour a day, five days a week. Contest-winning body builders who put on similar bulk, spend from five to seven hours a day, six to seven days a week, tussling with spine-crushing weights.

If you still desire big muscles, but not that large, you can gain them by doing Yogametrics ten minutes a day, five days a week. If you are satisfied, though, with acquiring a lean, hard, muscular figure with manly, youthful contours—or the type of figure which is most universally admired—you need to spend no more than 49 seconds a day with the well-guarded Yoga secret of two-second Yogametrics, as Charles did.

How 55-year-old Peter got to look younger and younger and enjoyed his retirement like a man 25 years his junior

Peter had worked steadily all his life, and had raised a family of three. He practically owned his own home now, had some money in the bank, owned some securities, and had a pension coming to him. He and his wife were eager to "see the world" at last, and reside for indefinite periods in different retirement paradises. But something troubled Peter. At 55 he looked like 64. By the time he retired, then, he would be like 74!

Since Peter still felt like a young man (except when he looked at himself in the mirror), it infuriated him to be viewed as a has-been. Under those circumstances, he concluded, retirement would be no fun at all for him. To keep right on working would be the lesser evil, for at the firm he was respected and looked up to by his young subordinates.

Peter revealed his problem to me and confessed that he wished he were still as young as I. When he learned my true age, his jaw dropped. "Why can't *I* look young, like *you*, doc?" He finally exclaimed. "Why don't *you* wrinkle, like me?"

"You don't have to keep your wrinkles," I told him. Then I revealed to him the Yoga secret of the Kavarzhan and how it makes faces youthful effortlessly by merely surrendering them *at specific angles* to the downpull of gravity.

Before the end of the week he called me up and told me that he had practiced the Kavarzhan twice and could already *feel* the wrinkles flattening out on his face while he did it.

I didn't see him again for three months. And then he looked ten years younger. When he retired, years later, he looked from 20 to 25 years younger than he was, and he wrote me from the Balearic Islands that he was enjoying himself "like a young man."

Eight years later Peter was still enjoying his retirement with relish, and he was past 70! "I just can't seem to look old anymore," he wrote me in utter amazement. "Kavarzhan rips old age from my face like a mask!"

How you, too, can look younger and younger with the Kavarzhan

You, too, can look younger and younger with the Kavarzhan and enjoy your retirement to the full. With it, you can also rise remarkably higher and more easily in social and business life by avoiding looking "too old," "past your prime," or "ready to kick the bucket." Such a look of perpetual youth has a decisive psychological impact upon you, both because of how differently others react to you, and because it keeps you still "in the competition." You never feel cast off or pitied, as a result, but always as if you are "one of the 'in' crowd."

These are only samples of the thousands of satisfying case histories that have resulted from applying the well-guarded Yoga secrets. Use them yourself and change your own life inside out—and it takes but seconds a day. This book will show you how.

Why You Need the Particular Benefits of Yoga

2

How your natural, inborn psychologic powers are being strangled

When you are born you enter the world without acquired fear, indecision, nervous tension, psychological complexes, envy, disappointments, frustrations, uncertainties or any of the other multitude of ego-crushing traits or attitudes. These life sappers reduce you to a miniscule of what you were originally mentally. One traumatic experience after another batters your ego around once you are out of your mother's womb, from the moment you are spanked to trigger your breathing, until nature snuffs the last spark of life from you. The natural psychological powers you were born with are progressively reduced to a shadow of what they were at first. You spend your whole life trying to regain their original might; but you are fortunate if you regain as much as a small fraction of them. Your brain, as a consequence, steadily loses much of its natural, inborn control over your body, and those two important parts of you become divorced from each other, like two independent relatives inhabiting the same house. You end up like the proverbial house divided against itself. With such an extensive loss of your natural, inborn psychologic powers, you degenerate into a faint image of the man you were born to be.

No acquisition can reward you more in life than your regaining as much as possible of your lost natural, inborn psychologic powers. These powers are still within your mind, but they are drastically suppressed. The Yogi has found out the secret of how to release them. That's why he can do things with his mind and body that baffle the world of science. Study his secrets and do likewise yourself.

Why Yoga will free your natural, inborn psychologic powers

The healthy mind helps the body, and the healthy body helps the mind. And Yoga is the union of the mind and body. You therefore need to use Yoga to free your natural, inborn psychologic powers because Yoga teaches you how to control your body with your mind. When, instead, you let your body control your mind, as Western man does, you become the slave of everything you feel or experience, whether it emanates from within you or from without.

Your natural, inborn psychologic powers are then crushed under a load of foreign impressions—of impressions foreign to your mind because they do not originate in it, but outside of it. And they are impressions which are not necessarily advantageous for you to receive or accept, for they saddle you with unnecessary psychological complexes and rob you of natural, inborn confidence in yourself (the confidence of the new-born babe). They make you shy and retiring, for instance, when you would otherwise be bold and masterful. They deflate you with pessimism, when you would otherwise burst with optimism. They imbue you with physical weakness, when you would otherwise stir with strength. They confuse your thinking and leave you negative, when you would otherwise think independently and be positive. They convert you into as inferior a person to your natural, inborn self as your everyday self is to your hypnotized self. Yoga takes your crushed, inferior, daily self and converts it *back into your natural, inborn self*: into the self in which your *mind* rules your body whenever you want it to.

Yoga restores your natural, inborn psychologic powers to you *not* through altering your mental attitudes, but through reopening wider the channels in your body through which your mind controls your body. These channels are your vertebral openings. Your spinal cord, which connects your brain to your body, sends its branches (your spinal nerves) to your body through these channels. When these channels are narrowed, as they become over the years as a result of these four horsemen, they squeeze your spinal nerves harder and weaken the power of the commands which your brain constantly sends to your body, consciously and subconsciously, through them. That, subconsciously, frustrates your brain and robs it of confidence to rule your body. By widening these narrowed channels, *Yoga enables your brain to send stronger commands to your body and regain lost power over it.* Your subconscious mind will be filled with lost confidence, and that, in turn, brings back to you lost natural, inborn psychologic powers.

The dim, unnoticed background constantly present in your consciousness

There is constantly present in your consciousness a sort of dim, unnoticed background consisting in great part of the impressions of your body sensations which your brain has recently received. These impressions are, normally, not vividly appreciated; but under abnormal conditions (such as when you suddenly face any strong competition), they may become the most vivid factors in your consciousness. If the body sensation which your brain has recently received is that of a vague, insignificant low back pain, for example, when you suddenly face any strong competition, your whole nervous system suffers a mild shock, and the vague, insignificant, hardly perceptible low back pain now pulses strongly in your conscious mind and routes your attitude of invincible optimism and supplants it with panicky feelings of fear and fatigue.

Possibilities of defeat at once flood into your consciousness, and you mentally alter into but one-third to one-tenth the man you were before. Your natural, inborn psychologic powers (your invincible confidence, optimism and unshakable determination) have vanished. All because of a hardly felt, meaningless ache in your lower back which you were hardly aware of before, but which suddenly triggered a train of defeat sensations in your consciousness. The well-guarded Yoga secrets were devised by the masters to enable them (and *you*, now) to meet and overcome any phenomena within the body that limit the full release of its natural, inborn psychologic powers, and to thereby let the *conscious mind* control the body, instead of the body controlling the mind.

Your spinal cord—the pathway of control between your brain and body

All messages from your *body to your brain*, either conscious or subconscious, and all commands from your conscious or subconscious *minds to your body*, are transmitted through your spinal cord (except those which go directly from your brain to your head or face). Every message and command is transmitted along a nerve and through your spinal cord in the form of nerve electricity, which is received at its destination and decoded. Any obstacle along the course of the nerve will reduce the voltage of its nerve electricity and lessen the clarity and intensity of the message or command it is transmitting.

These facts are of utmost importance because the variety of messages or commands which can be transmitted between your brain and body are without limit, since they are capable of describing anything and everything that is impressed upon them, from the most concrete to the most imaginary. Indeed, the total number of nerve cells to be found in the outer, gray covering of your brain (which houses your conscious and subconscious minds) and which receive or transmit messages or commands between your brain or body, has been estimated at around ten billion (or 10^{10})! And the number of nerve cables which convey these messages or commands between the cells and your body total in the neighborhood of 200,000.

In addition to that, there are many times more nerve cables than these, which convey messages or commands in your brain *itself* between its different nerve cells, or which relate different areas of your brain with others. They explain why *every function* of your body can be related to every other function in it, through your brain and nervous system.

Your vertebral openings—the channels through which your spinal cord branches into your body to transmit messages or commands between your brain and body

The nerve electricity flowing through the different nerve pathways in your spinal cord, either from your brain to your body,

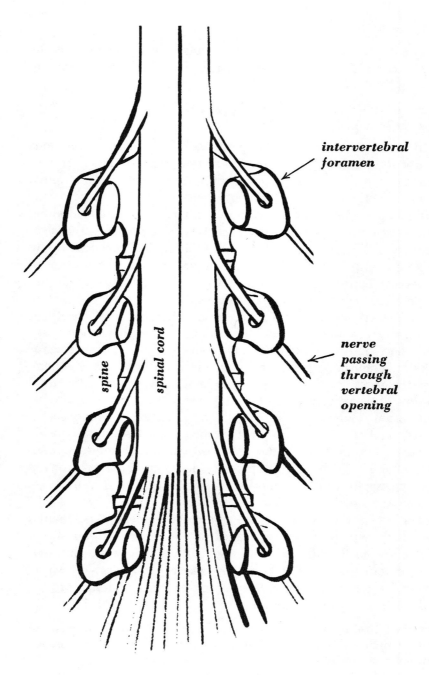

intervertebral foramen

nerve passing through vertebral opening

spine

spinal cord

Figure 1
Spine Sliced in Half Lengthwise

or from your body to your brain, has to pass through the vertebral openings in your spine in order to reach their destination (*Figure 1*). Your vertebrae are cylindrical bones with 'back tails" and "side handles" (*Figure 2*). They stand one above the other, like stacked up bricks, and compose your spine. Your spine is the axis implanted in the middle of your back, extending upwards from your hips to your skull. It acts as a protecting case for your delicate spinal cord, which fits in it like a sword in its sheath (*Figure 2*). One-fourth of your spine consists of spinal disks or cushions, which are sandwiched between the individual vertebrae. Your spinal disks cushion any weight, pressure or strain on your spine, such as when you bend or twist or engage in any other physical activity. Strongly resistant ligaments envelop and bind your vertebrae together and keep them in their places and in a vertiçal line with each other. Strong, active back muscles support the ligaments. Your vertebrae form joints with their neighbors above and below them because the spinal disks between them are elastic and allow them a certain degree of movement.

Each vertebra has an opening on each side of it, formed by part of its base and part of the top of the vertebra below it (*Figure 2*). Through these openings, a right and left branch of your spinal cord (your spinal nerves) pass into your body (*Figure 1*). Other structures also pass through your vertebral openings, such as the arteries which carry blood to your vertebrae, the veins which remove the metabolic wastes of the vertebrae, and your sympathetics, which directly rule your blood circulation. Since the branches of your spinal cord passing through your vertebral openings control all the functions of your body, the contents of your vertebral openings have been termed the life-line, or the vital passages of your body. Without your vertebral openings as a means of access, your brain and body could not communicate with each other, and all your body functions would come to a stop. Hardly any part of your anatomy is more important for your normal health, or even for your life itself, than your vertebral openings.

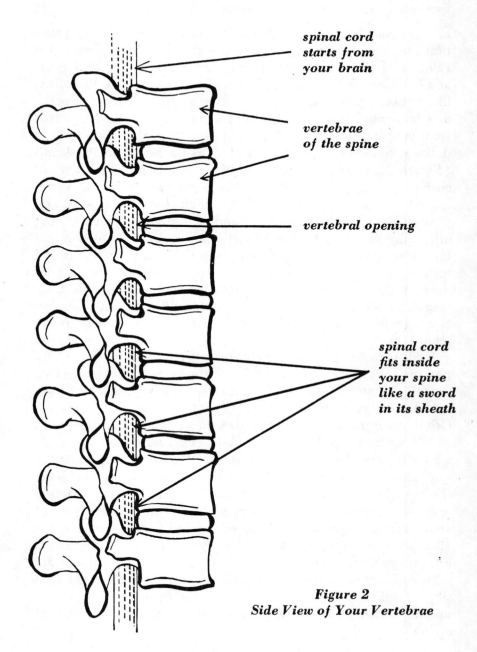

spinal cord starts from your brain

vertebrae of the spine

vertebral opening

spinal cord fits inside your spine like a sword in its sheath

Figure 2
Side View of Your Vertebrae

all the different nerve pathways have to pass through the vertebral openings in your spine on the way to their destinations

How your vertebral openings are hammered down and narrowed by the relentless pounding of the four horsemen of the mastabah

Your vertebral openings, unfortunately, possess deadly enemies in the four horsemen of the mastabah. The most vicious attacker of the four is your faulty posture and the resulting faulty body mechanics. And, unfortunately, you *don't* inherit good body posture. Other animals inherit it, but man does not because, since he adopted a two-legged stance, all parts of his body necessary for good posture are *not complete* at birth. (His pyramidal nervous system, for example, which delivers the commands from his brain to his muscles to assume and balance him in the two-legged posture is one.) And so, man, of all vertebrates, stands and walks at later periods of life than other animals. Consequently, he has to be trained to stand and walk by himself. It's not instinctively acquired by civilized man.

You obtain good body mechanics *only* when all the joints of your body enjoy "a safety range of motion" and suffer the least possible grinding friction within them from any strain by gravity, posture, locomotion, weight-bearing or ground resistance. With the passing years, though, the relentless pounding of the four horsemen of the mastabah pushes down your spine, distorting it with wrong-back curves and throwing groups of vertebrae out of line. Any wrong-back curve, mild or otherwise, reduces your good body mechanics and throws undue strain upon different joints of your body. It limits the safety range of motion of those joints, and increases the traumas they receive from the stresses and strains which they endure from these four pounding horsemen. That is an anatomical catastrophe because your spine responds to every move you make (even when you are merely breathing or lying down resting), and your whole back can be incapacitated when *just one* vertebra is markedly out of line with the rest. Actually, all the vertebrae of *no* spine always sit perfectly in line upon, or below, one another. There always exists some degree (even if symptomless and subclinical) of low-grade "off-centering" of one or more vertebrae (*Figure 3*). And, it limits to a varying degree the freedom of your normal back movements, such as bending forwards, backwards, twisting and so on, and strains to a varying degree the ligaments and muscles which hold your "off-centered" vertebrae in place. When this off-centering of different vertebrae is caused by the relentless pounding of the four horsemen of the mastabah, the unfortunate vertebrae are gradually hammered out of shape over the years, and their openings narrowed. Less space then remains for their contents to pass out from your spine through them. Even the openings of vertebrae that remain in line with each other are narrowed besides because the four pounding horsemen of the mastabah wear down and thin the spinal disks sandwiched between them, jamming the neighboring vertebrae closer to each other and hence narrowing the openings they form between them.

How your narrowed vertebral openings convert your spinal cord into an energy-starved mass of nerve segments

As a result of the constant subclinical (non-painful, non-diagnostic) pressure which your narrowed vertebral openings apply upon their contents, the blood vessels passing through them are partly flattened, as occurs when you step upon a hose. Thus, they convey less oxygen and nutrition and disease-resisting lymph to your spinal cord, and also carry away less metabolic wastes from it. Your victimized spinal cord, as a consequence, degenerates gradually into a blood-starved, lymph-starved, energy-starved mass of nerve segments. Your nerve fibers, which are the units of your spinal cord, require a steady supply of blood in order to retain their capacity to manufacture nerve-electricity and transmit messages and commands along their lengths, to your brain and body. They cannot do so long without oxygen. Constant subclinical pressure on the blood vessels which bring oxygen to your nerve fibers will steadily lessen the voltage of their nerve-electricity (their Spino-Volt) and thereby weaken the intensity of the messages which they carry from your body *to* your brain, and of the commands which they deliver *from* your brain to your body.

Your blood, besides, neutralizes the acids which your cells produce when they function. When the nerves of your spinal cord receive less blood than normal, the acids of their metabolic waste-products accumulate in them. That leaves them *super*-sensitive to the messages they receive, and so they overexcite your mind with their messages and incline you to react to them abnormally and aberrantly, like a mild hysteric. For that same reason, too, your nerves alternately turn numb from acid fatigue,

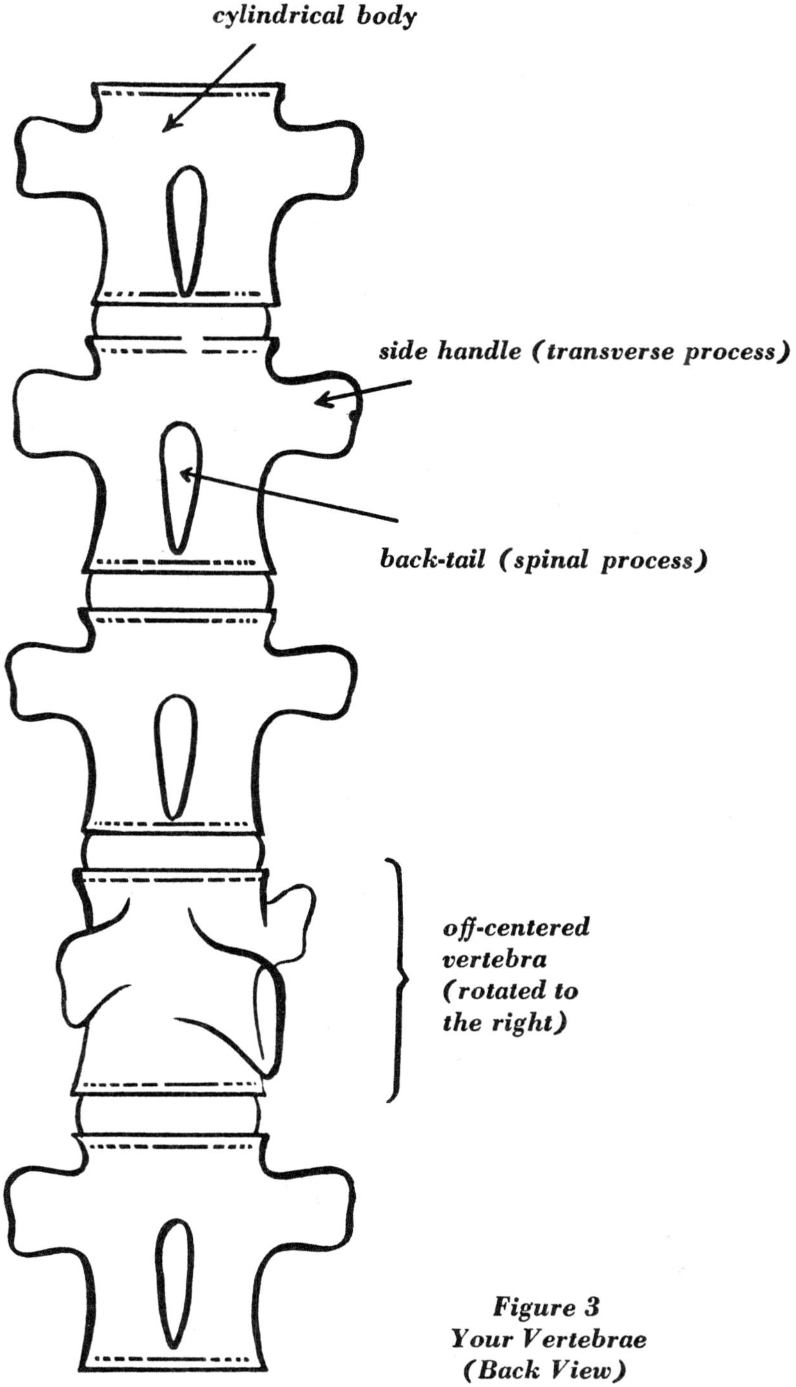

cylindrical body

side handle (transverse process)

back-tail (spinal process)

off-centered
vertebra
(rotated to
the right)

Figure 3
Your Vertebrae
(Back View)

and then transmit their messages or commands vaguely and weakly.

Starved for enough blood, lymph and energy-producing nutrition, your spinal cord is gradually converted into a prematurely aging, increasingly devitalized, transmitting mass of feebly responding nerve pathways.

How your narrowed vertebral openings decrease the natural, inborn influence of your brain and body over each other

All nerves consist of nerve fibers. And since a nerve fiber is of semi-fluid consistency, any slight pressure on a nerve (such as on any of your spinal nerves) will change its protoplasmic continuity and hinder the normal flow of its nerve-electricity over the rest of its length and weaken the drive of the messages it carries to your brain, or of the commands it delivers to your body. When the slight pressure is removed, your nerve again transmits messages or commands with its normal drive. When the sciatic nerve of the frog is stimulated by an electric current, for example, its gastrocnemius (leg) muscle contracts. When pressure is applied on that nerve, though, the gastrocnemius muscle of the frog does not contract. The experiment demonstrates that enough pressure may be applied to a nerve to *prevent it* from transmitting messages or commands *without destroying* the nerve itself.

You can demonstrate that on yourself. Cross one leg over the other and sit still for a while. The resulting pressure upon the nerves of one, or both, legs, will cause one, or both, of them to turn numb. The same thing happens when you hit your "funny bone" (or the ulnar nerve coursing through your elbow).

When similar pressure is applied to a spinal nerve of yours by the squeeze of the narrowed vertebral opening through which it passes, it does not crush or injure the spinal nerve. But it *lessens* the nerve-electricity of that nerve when it carries a message from your body to your brain, or when it delivers a command from your brain to your body. Your brain will, as a consequence, receive *weaker* messages from your body, and your body will receive *weaker* commands from your brain. Their natural, inborn influence over each other will be decreased—and markedly so with time. Dire results will follow in your brain and body as you grow older, without your even suspecting them . . . dire results which cut short your youth, longevity, sex potency, manly sex appeal, energy, muscle strength, memory, confidence, popularity, power of leadership and of everything else that means anything to you. The well-guarded Yoga secrets were begotten by the Yogis to prevent such dire results from taking place in them. Learn how you, too, can prevent them *scientifically* with these secrets.

How to Regain Your Natural, Inborn, Manly Powers with Yoga

3

Over the years, the continual pressure exerted both upon your spinal and your sympathetic nerves by the squeeze of your narrowed vertebral openings on them, diminishes markedly the natural inborn powers and influence of your brain and body over each other. Of all tissues, to repeat, those of your brain and spinal cord are the most easily injured when their oxygen supply is reduced, as occurs when your blood-circulation-controlling sympathetic nerves are squeezed. Your narrowed vertebral openings, for that reason, are the direct causes of the varied, confusing, bewildering frustrating and sneaky vague pains you experience periodically, and these bring on the subclinical (unfelt, undiagnostic) symptoms of pseudo-hardening of the arteries and shorten your natural inborn lifespan. Arteriosclerosis and atherosclerosis, or hardening and narrowing of the arteries, restrict the normal amount of blood circulating through them. The narrowing of your vertebral openings produces more or less similar, but subclinical, symptoms, by weakening the normal power of the nerve-electricity of your sympathetic nerves to widen and narrow the arteries of your body and propel the blood through them.

That affects *all* the organs or structures of your body by undernourishing them and allowing their waste products to accumulate in them, thereby reducing their efficiency and their resistance to disease. Your muscles, as a result, lose tone and strength, and your digestive tract loses peristaltic powers. The net result in you is a pseudo-functional or subclinical arteriosclerosis (similar to a hardening of the arteries). The condition is characterized by a loss of elasticity of the walls of your arteries, because the muscles of their walls now possess less contractile power.

In the arteries of your brain the pseudo-hardening brings on hardly perceptible, but brain power reducing, symptoms of forgetfulness, confusion and personality changes commonly seen in elderly persons. In the absence of other causes, those above 45 years old, with marked narrowing of the vertebral openings, are inclined to show prematurely graying hair; poor growth or roughening of the finger- and toe-nails; loss of the normal healthy appearance of the skin and loss of substance of the muscles, especially of the legs, and early signs of slowing down of the blood circulation in the legs. The appetite lessens, and the digestion is "not so good anymore." All of it leads to a subchronic state of malnutrition and subclinical cirrhosis of the liver, because less protein, specifically choline, as well as less of all other foods, is now absorbed.

The kidneys, heart, spleen, brain and nervous system, all now shrink to a slight degree, as if you were partly starving yourself. They therefore assimilate less of the daily required vitamins, minerals and nutrients which they need to function normally. Your heart muscle consequently, is supplied with less calcium, and your brain and spinal cord with less cephalin. Your reflexes, as a result, are slower, and constipation sets in from the constant, subchronic, but minutely increasing indigestion. Skin diseases may ensue from the resulting growth changes, because of the slowed blood circulation to your skin. Your special senses deteriorate faster than they should, too, with your sight and hearing leading the parade. Your adrenal glands try to restore some of your steadily decreasing body tone by faintly speeding up your heart, but thereby also tending to raise your blood pressure. From head to foot you present a symptomless, subclinical picture of obviously "getting older and older," or that of a mild, but similar picture, of hardening of the arteries.

Physiologically you acquire, from it all, a lowered vitality (or reduced body resistance) which leaves you more prone to infections; more prone to such chronic diseases as arthritis; to degenerative changes within the tissues of your bones, muscles and ligaments; to a tendency to chronic old-age ailments, like diabetes, liver and kidney trouble; and possibly, to a greater tendency to cancer, heart and artery afflictions. Your natural, inborn lifespan, obviously, is shortened.

Your narrowed vertebral openings, in brief, bring about unwanted structural alterations in you, and these are due almost completely to the relentless pounding of the four horsemen of the mastabah.

How widening your narrowed vertebral openings restores sufficient and natural inborn powers and counteracts the effects of pseudo-hardening of your arteries

Your narrowed vertebral openings prevent you from using your full, natural, inborn psychologic powers, too, because both your conscious and subconscious minds function best only when your body can be used with no strain on any of its parts . . . no strain that lessens your natural, inborn confidence in yourself; your natural, inborn optimism; your natural, inborn courage, and all the other invincible attitudes which you naturally possessed at birth. It means that, when you sit, stand or engage in any activity, your body should be held in a proper, balanced position, with its normal spinal curves (to be revealed later) always in control of its center of gravity, and with no unnecessary strain exerted on your joints, bones, ligaments, muscles, or on any other structures. Your rib box should be predominantly set in positions which allow room for your stomach, intestines, liver, kidneys, urinary bladder, colon, spleen—all your visceral organs in fact—to perform their natural functions as normally as possible. Your muscles will then be properly balanced against each other, instead of some of them being chronically tightly contracted (or thrown into muscle spasm), while their antagonist muscles are over-relaxed and flaccid. Your vertebral openings will then be normally wide enough not to squeeze their contents harder and to let your spinal cord transmit messages and commands charged with their full nerve-electricity (their full Spino-Volt). You cannot attain that ideal state if your spine is twisted or distorted in a fixed position by off-centered vertebrae; your head held too far forward, or backward, or to one side; your abdomen regularly protruding like a balloon and throwing your visceral organs out of place; or your feet allowed to flatten more and point outwards as you move or walk.

Fortunately, the Yoga secrets are especially begotten to discourage those physical distortions from forming on your body, or to remove or relieve them as much as possible after they are formed, by molding you into using all the mechanical parts of your body in a scientific manner that throws the least possible strain on any of its parts. The Yoga secrets achieve that goal because your spine is a flexible rod made up of segments, and it changes considerably during the 24-hour period (*Figure 4*). The

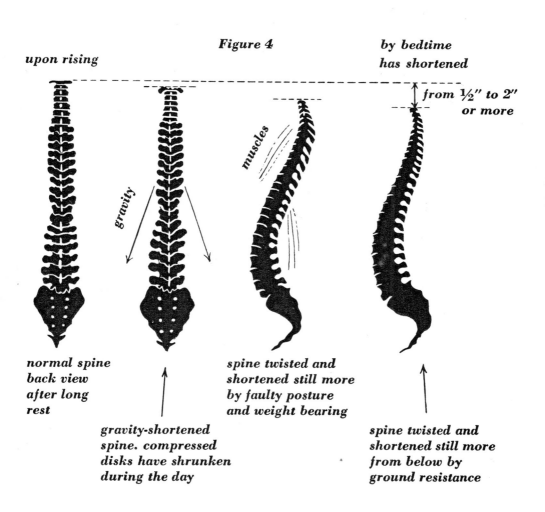

Figure 4

upon rising

*by bedtime
has shortened*

*from ½" to 2"
or more*

*normal spine
back view
after long
rest*

*spine twisted and
shortened still more
by faulty posture
and weight bearing*

*gravity-shortened
spine. compressed
disks have shrunken
during the day*

*spine twisted and
shortened still more
from below by
ground resistance*

entire philogenetic history of man, in fact, from his childhood on, is the history of a never-ending struggle against the relentless down-pull of gravity. With the aid of habitual faulty posture, weight-bearing and ground resistance, gravity deforms your daily posture and hammers down and narrows your vertebral openings and brings on the life-shortening effects of pseudo-hardening of the arteries. Widening your narrowed vertebral openings with the Yoga secrets restores most, if not all, of the natural, inborn powers to your spinal cord and counteracts the life-shortening effects on you of pseudo-hardening of your arteries.

How widening your narrowed vertebral openings removes pressure from your spinal (and sympathetic) nerves and restores their vitality

As stated before, the messages which arise in your body and are sent to your brain, and the commands which are fashioned in your brain and dispatched to your body, are transmitted to their respective destinations by means of your spinal cord and its branches, your spinal nerves. And since these nerves pass through your vertebral openings, when these openings are narrowed the Spino-Volts of the spinal nerves are reduced, and the intensity of the messages or commands they transmit is weakened.

Why? Because the physiological maintenance of a nerve depends upon nerve movements. Nerve peristalsis or movements amount to a continual delivery of fresh energizing material (cytoplasm) throughout the whole nerve (*Figure 5*). It is elaborated in the nerve cell (or where the nerve segment of the spinal nerve begins, just inside the vertebral opening), and it is propelled in a peristaltic manner by the nerve body, along its entire length—including those of all its branches—to the very termination of the nerve in some organ, gland or other tissue. Nerve peristalsis supplies the nerve and all its parts with components that are used to maintain the nerve and its activity. The total volume of cytoplasm synthesized by the nerve cell is considerable, and it may be replaced several times each day.

How counteracting the merciless battering of the four horsemen improves, relieves or sometimes cures a great many afflictions

When you counteract the merciless battering of the four pounding horsemen with the well-guarded Yoga secrets, you will improve, relieve or cure a number of afflictions in your body. You

Figure 5

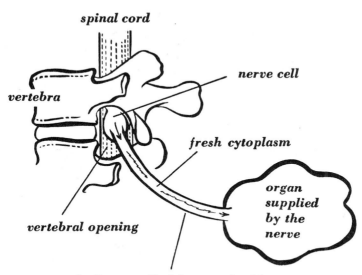

spinal cord

nerve cell

vertebra

fresh cytoplasm

organ supplied by the nerve

vertebral opening

nerve body propelled in a peristaltic manner

will be taught Yoga secrets for constipation, hemorrhoids, fatigue, backaches, varicose veins. Yoga secrets for arthritis, foot trouble, stiff joints and muscles, and for easing the load of the heart, prostate, hernia, sacroiliac. Yoga secrets, for wrinkles, crows feet, overweight, underweight, acquired spinal distortions, general malaise, stomach and intestinal disorders. Yoga secrets for muscular arms, strong legs, broad shoulders, manificent chest, strong heart, strong V-shaped back, trim waist, strong neck. Yoga secrets for flexible spine, sex power, nervous tension, age-controlling glands, sub-clinical diabetes, lumbago, rheumatism, headaches. Also, Yoga secrets for inventiveness, originality, longevity, popularity, leadership, for the executive and professional man, energy, self-mastery, sex appeal, re-elongating the height. Yoga secrets for concentration, memory, banishing disease, staying young longer, defying old age, strengthening the subconscious mind's control over body functions, and much else. So, start learning these well-guarded secrets now as they appear in the following pages.

Yoga Secrets for Sex Appeal

4

The Yogi is very proud of the appeal of his personal self, which is tantamount to his sex appeal. He devotes much of his practice to perfecting it. The Yogi declares that his body then pleases his mind more, and is accepted by it for union. His well-guarded secrets of what amount to sex appeal have therefore been carefully studied and scientifically refined for *your own* use, to enable you to gain the utmost from them fast, without resorting to long disciplines or other unwise straining of your body. The case histories at the end prove how effective they can be for you also.

How the four horsemen of the mastabah deplete your natural, inborn sex appeal

The four horsemen of the mastabah (gravity, faulty posture, weight-bearing and ground resistance) deplete your natural, in-born sex appeal by battering down your body through:

1. Overworking your anti-gravity muscles.
2. Adding wrong curves to your back which destroy your grace of movements.
3. Creating distorted pictures to others of your true personality, through the misleading visual impressions of you which your wrong back curves create.

4. The compressive pushdown strain of postural weight-bearing on your back, shoulders, joints and spinal disks.

5. The relentless downpull of gravity, which affects every part of you, from birth to the grave—particularly, when you sit or stand—narrowing your shoulders, drooping them, and sapping the tone of your abdominal wall.

You will now be shown how the four horsemen of the mastabah bring on those unwanted changes in you and reduce your natural, inborn sex appeal, and the refined, scientifically perfected Yoga secrets for your counteracting them and gaining the utmost benefits from them in your life, as swiftly as possible.

How your overworked anti-gravity muscles rob you of your natural, inborn sex appeal

Due to the relentless downpull of gravity and the narrow base of support of your body by your feet, your body in the erect position is unstable and sways constantly. If this swaying were not limited by the contractions of the muscles of the outsides of your calves and of the fronts of your thighs (or by the muscles which straighten your knees) your legs would buckle at the hips, knees and ankles, and you would fall. But your body sway stretches these muscles and their tendons, and so causes them to contract continuously. When gravity no longer stretches them, such as when you are lying down, their continuous contractions stop. For that reason, the muscles of the outsides of your calves and of the fronts of your thighs—as well as your abdominal muscles and the muscles of your lower back—are called the *anti-gravity muscles*. They, consequently, possess the most muscle tone of all your muscles.

Combatting gravity hour after hour wearies you, even when you just stand idly. The muscles of your triceps, of your chest and of the sides of your neck, in contrast, are less firm than your anti-gravity muscles because they are in use mainly when the parts they support are used. Your anti-gravity muscles, however, have to be well toned in order to help out your heart; for gravity, when you are standing, draws the blood down from your heart into your legs and feet, but afterwards it tries to *prevent* the same blood from flowing back up to your lungs and heart via your muscle-less veins.

Your anti-gravity muscles, though, automatically help your pumping heart to overcome the opposing downpull of gravity by squeezing the veins in your legs and squirting the pooling blood in them back up to your lungs and heart. When you stand motionless for a long time, however, your anti-gravity muscles practically cramp and squeeze the capillaries and small veins of your legs so tightly that now they severely *impede* the blood flow back to your lungs and heart and cause your heart to overwork instead. That explains why standing motionless fatigues you much sooner than rhythmical walking. Since you spend so much time every day standing still, you therefore fatigue more than you normally should. Your sex appeal, as a result, deserts you to a marked degree because women admire most the man who does not look fatigued but virile. When you are fatigued, besides, you lose confidence in yourself; you lose optimism and other aggressive qualities. All of this depletes your natural, inborn psychologic powers. Your sex appeal is reduced still more for that reason. Since you cannot alter the feminine instinctive impression of man, you have to take the bull by the horns and tone up your anti-gravity muscles. Do so effectively with Yogatone.

How to tone up your anti-gravity muscles with Yogatone

Figure 6A: Lie flat on back, with palms down at your sides.
Figure 6B: (1) Point toes and
              (2) Contract calves. Then
              (3) Contract fronts of thighs by pressing down hard on bed with your heels (3A).
              (4) Hump over as if trying to look at your toes, and
              (5) Contract abdominal muscles.
              (6) Bring hands close together and
              (7) Round your shoulders.

              Hold for 2 seconds. Then relax. Do it 1–10 times a day, depending on how fast you want results.

NOTE: Satisfactorily toned anti-gravity muscles are also most important for restoring your natural, inborn sex appeal because they add a subtle spring to your step, and help you assume and maintain a manly posture which stamps you with thrilling sex appeal.

Figure 6
How to Tone Up Your Anti-Gravity Muscles with Yogatone

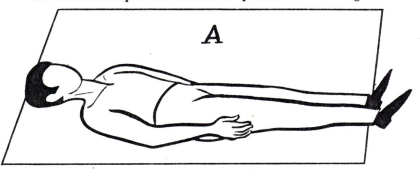

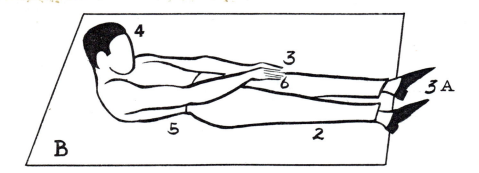

**How the wrong-back curves steadily diminish
your natural, inborn Spino-Volt power**

Any wrong-back curve diminishes your manly sex appeal because it narrows still more the vertebral openings in it; as a
result, they squeeze still harder the spinal nerves passing through
them and lessen their Spino-Volt power.

Do not confuse your wrong-back curves, though, with your
natural, *correct* back curves. In order to resist effectively the
merciless battering of the four horsemen of the mastabah, your
back needs its four natural, correct back curves (*Figure 7—A*).
These four curves are not accidental. On the contrary, they help
your spine resist the ceaseless punishment of these four horsemen.
In order to do so:

1. Your correct back curves contribute to the strength of your spine. (The normally curved spine is approximately 16 times stronger than if it were completely straight.)
2. Your correct back curves convert your spine into an elastic structure which provides a springy pillar upon which your head can rest, thereby minimizing the danger of severely jarring your brain from the traumas of ground resistance, sudden jolts, or any other activity.
3. Your correct back curves are so arranged as to favor the housing of your organs, for they immensely enlarge your chest cavity (or rib box), or the space where your heart, lungs and other important body structures are contained.
4. Your correct back curves arch gradually enough to prevent the possibility of compression of your spinal cord, which might occur if any abrupt angles were formed by your spine along its length.

Figure 7—A is a sketch of the ideal back with the four natural, correct back curves, viewed from the side of the body. Your masculine spine is about 71 cm. long, or about 10 cm. longer than the female's on the average. You possess one natural, correct back curve in your neck, one in the torso region of your back, one in your lower back, and one on the back of your hips. Due to these curves, the center of gravity of your body (or the point in your body where your body is balanced with the downpull of gravity) is a trifle below your lower back (or, technically, at the level of your second sacral segment).

Over the years, though, the incessant hammering of the four horsemen of the mastabah wears down your spinal disks to varying degrees, shifting many of your vertebrae slightly off the center line of your spine (or "off-centering" them) and misshaping your back, and therefore either lessening or exaggerating your natural, correct back curves (*Figure 7—B, C, D*). With this "distorting" of your spine, the bodies (cylindrical portions) of your vertebrae no longer carry your entire weight, but dump part of it upon their tail-halves, as well as upon the side-handles of the last vertebra of your lower back, the all-important trouble-causing fifth lumbar vertebra. Those changes alter every move you make. As your natural, correct back curves deepen in your neck and lower back and become *wrong*-back curves, the weight in the

Figure 7
Correct and Wrong-Back Curves

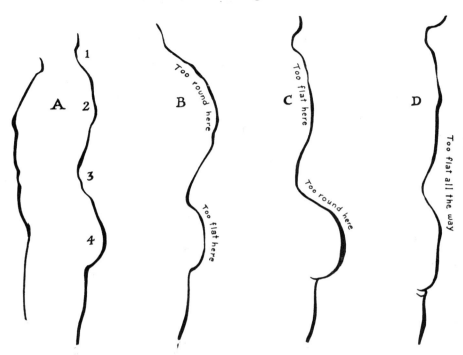

A   **normal back with the four correct back curves**
B   **kyphotic back**
C   **lordotic back**
D   **weak, flat back**

torso-region of your back is also shifted from its normal resting place squarely upon the cylindrical bodies of the vertebrae there, to the more *forward parts* of their cylindrical bodies. Your cylindrical vertebral bodies, though, are porous and comparatively fragile; hence, the abnormal weight which their anterior parts carry now, gradually compresses them into wedge-shaped bodies (*Figure 8*).

That narrows your vertebral openings still more and places the torso-region of your back under continuous stress and strain.

Figure 8

*bodies of
vertebrae
and spinal
discs are
normal*

*bodies of
vertebrae
compressed
into wedge-
shaped bodies*

The range of the bending, twisting and turning movements of your torso is obviously limited thereafter. This condition may be more pronounced if your torso-back is rounding out backwards more and more into a wrong-back curve (Kyphosis) (*Figure 7—B*).

These forming wrong-back curves will bend your spinal cord, which is encased in your spine, unduly and diminish its Spino-Volt and consequently lessen the intensity of the messages it is carrying from your body to your brain, and of the commands it is delivering from your brain to your body (*Figure 9*).

**How your wrong-back curves present (to women, especially)
a distorted and unflattering conception of your true
personality and sex appeal**

Your wrong-back curves also reduce sharply your sex appeal by presenting distorted, unflattering pictures of your true person-

Figure 9

normal back

mild wrong-back curves

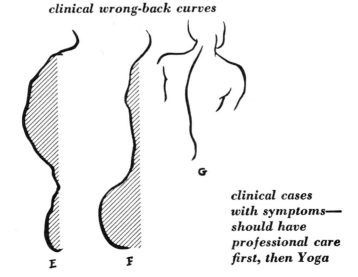

A

mildly rounded torso back

B

mildly deepened lower-back curve

C

D

postural lateral curvature (no structural changes evident on X-rays)

subclinical symptomless— can be corrected with Yoga alone

clinical wrong-back curves

E

F

G

clinical cases with symptoms— should have professional care first, then Yoga ality, especially to women. Thus, they compel you instinctively to waste energy in trying to erase from their minds those erroneous conceptions of you which they adopt. Your unexplainable loss of former sex appeal also confuses you, even if subconsciously, and reduces further your natural, inborn psychologic powers. Here is specifically how the wrong-back curves do it.

Kyphosis. If your wrong-back curve consists of a deeply out-curving torso-back (*Figure 7—B*), you look decidedly shorter than you are, depending upon the acuteness of the curve. Such a curve also tends to give you an inelegant thick-set look, because it brings your chest and your waistline closer together and thickens your torso from front to back. Your head hangs lower, lending you a slightly slow-witted look. The sharp, keen, commanding aspect of the leader is something no one will see in you, and women classify you more as a kind-hearted, good-natured person who is very likely a good provider, but certainly not romantic. Your sex appeal, in other words, has vanished.

Lordosis. If your wrong-back curve consists of a deeply in-curving lower back with jutting hips (*Figure 7–C*), you look juvenile, depending upon the depth of the incurve. It fixes the woman's attention on the prominence of your hips instead of on your chest and shoulders, where it should be placed, and inclines her subconsciously to compare you to boys instead of concentrating on you as the "he-man" she would admire. As you walk, besides, such positioned hips tend to sway from side-to-side more than is expected of a man, lessening still more your expected virile, masculine aspect. With your head thrown backwards as it is, too, to balance your protruding hips against the imbalancing downpull of gravity, you instinctively walk and swing your arms like the cock-of-the-walk. No matter how modest you may be, the woman is sure to regard you as insufferably conceited and treat you with disdain. You will really have to strain to overcome such an impression, once she gets it.

Scoliosis. If your wrong-back curve is a sideways one with uneven shoulders (*Figure 9—A*), you tend to walk with your head leaning to the side of the low shoulder. The picture suggests a bully or a low-brow.

When your wrong-back curves are not pronounced, these effects on women will be less pointed, but they might influence them enough to elicit from them a different reaction than you expected, especially before you meet them or before they know you well, and undermine your best efforts with them.

The visual impression you make on women with any of the wrong-back curves is negative because oxygen tensions are evoked in the brain by visual stimulation. But when you present the *right picture* of yourself to the woman you want, or the picture of yourself which *you want* her to get, her brain acquires greater nerve-tone. The mere sight of you—*before you even breathe a word*—excites her then. Achieve that power over her by lessening your wrong-back curves.

How to lessen your wrong-back curves with Yogametrics

How to Lessen a Kyphotic Back. The
Lower Back Doorway Pull

The position to assume (Figure 10—A)

1. Stand close to the free end of an opened door, facing it squarely.
2. Grasp, with your fingers alone, the door-knobs on each side of it.
3. Let your body drop backwards, back straight, until
4. Your arms are straight.
5. Your legs are straight too, so that your whole body is straight.

How to do this simple movement (Figure 10—B)

1. Round your shoulders. (Turn them inwards, downwards and backwards.) (*Figure 10–C*)
2. Inhale deeply as you pull your still straight body towards the door, with your fingers. At the same time
3. Arch your back, and drop your weight backwards.
4. Hug your body tightly with your elbows.
5. You will rise up on your toes, as the movement progresses. If you are tall, bend your knees a little.
6. Keep your shoulders rounded all the while, with
7. Your elbows still hugging your body until the end.

Hold the contraction, at the end, for two seconds. Then relax.

This simple movement develops (Figure 10–D):

1. The lower portion of your latissimus dorsi (*Figure 10–*

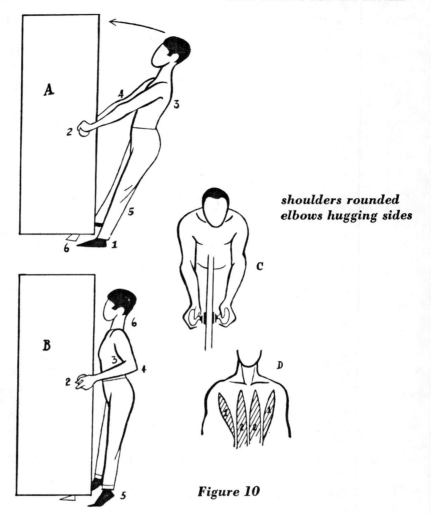

*shoulders rounded
elbows hugging sides*

Figure 10

D–1). Indeed, you actually feel the muscle tearing right off your body, it contracts so hard.

2. Your sacrospinalis (*Figure 10–D–2*), the muscles that give your back that deep groove in the lower half, and straightens it and gives you "the romantic look." Easy, simple, but phenomenal simple movement.

Frequency:

1–10 times a day, depending on how fast you want results.

*To keep strain off the hinges, place a small wedge under the bottom of the free end of the door (*Figure 10–A–6*).

How to Lessen Your Scoliotic Wrong-Back Curve with the Doorway Side Stretch

The position to assume (Figure 11–A)

1. Stand close to, and facing, the free end of an opened door.
2. Grasp *each half* of the top corner of it with the fingers of each hand, so that your opposite *fingers meet.*

How to do this simple movement (Figure 11–B)

3. Pull down hard with your hands, to lift your shoulders.
4. If your right shoulder is the lower shoulder, raise your left foot to lengthen the leg, and

Figure 11

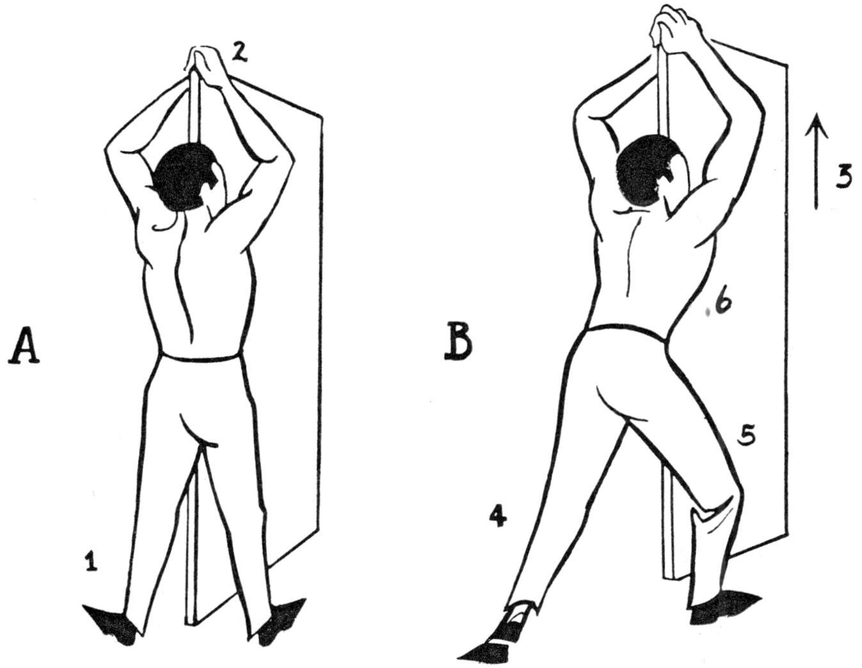

5. Bend your right knee and drop your weight on your right foot, to

6. Stretch your right side and straighten your wrong-back curve.

Hold the position for two seconds. Do it from 1–10 times a day, depending on how fast you want results.

*(If your left shoulder is the low one, do No. 4 with your right foot, and Nos. 5 and 6 with your left knee and foot, and thus stretch your *left* side and straighten your wrong-back curve.)

HOW TO LESSEN YOUR LORDOTIC WRONG-BACK CURVE

You lessen your lordotic wrong-back curve by toning up your abdominal muscles with the Abdominal Curl.

The Abdominal Curl

Lie flat on your back, with your arms along sides, or on top of thighs. Raise head and try to see the floor between your feet. Then try to see it between your knees; then between your thighs (*Figure 12*).

Figure 12

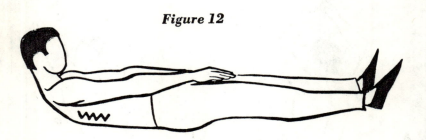

How to square and broaden your shoulders with minimum effort

Since all instinctively admire the man with broad shoulders, you can't afford to let yours droop and look narrower than they are naturally. Fortunately, they can even be broadened *beyond* their natural appearance, because the tendons of your shoulder muscles which form cuffs around your shoulder joints, can be stretched a *full inch out* from each shoulder. By toning up your trapezius muscles afterwards, you easily hold up your broadened shoulders, like a clothes rack, and their new width will be noticed by all—particularly, by the woman you want to impress. Widening your shoulder joint, besides, improves the blood circulation of the joint by keeping the joint well-lubricated. It also strengthens the ligaments and tendons of the joint, and is most helpful in preventing and overcoming bursitis of the shoulder, which is a common ailment. It also enables you to escape being saddled with the narrow, shrinking shoulders of past middle- and old-age, and consequently keeps you looking appealing all your life.

THE TWO-ARM DOORWAY STRETCH, THE SHOULDER-BROADENER AND WAIST THINNER (THE YOGI SPREAD)

Figure 13

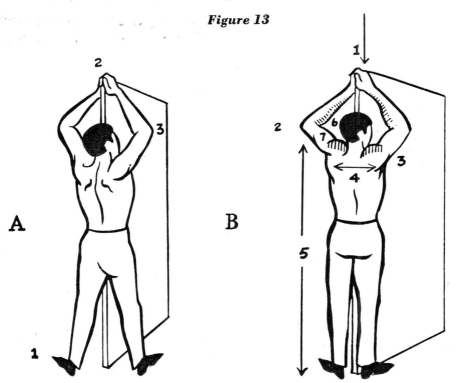

The position to assume (Figure 13—A)

1. Stand close to the free end of an opened door, facing it. (Closet door should do.)

2. Place tips of fingers of each hand on its corresponding half of the top edge of the door. If you are too short, stand on a chair, a solid box or a secure stool.

3. Elbows somewhat bent, and pointed directly outwards.

How to do this simple movement (Figure 13—B)

1. Pull down hard with the tips of your fingers.
2. Your elbows will point outwards farther;
3. Your shoulders will be drawn high, and will
4. Raise and spread your shoulder blades wider apart, thus broadening your shoulders. Hold for two seconds.
5. Your waist will be thinned, because your torso will be pulled upwards from above (by your arms), and pulled downwards from below (by the weight of your hips and legs).

This simple movement:

1. Broadens your shoulders, and
2. Lengthens (stretches) and slims down your side-to-side waistline profile. A remarkably simple movement to bring back to you—and retain—"that sex appeal look." It also develops the under side of the forearm (*Figure 13—B—6*), as well as the Trapezius (1st section) (*Figure 13—B—7*).

Frequency

1–4 times a day, depending on how fast you want results.

THE TWO-ARM DOORWAY STRETCH FOR
PREVENTING OR COMBATING BURSITIS

1. Assume the same position as in *Figure 13—A*, facing the door.
2. Pick up your sore arm with your sound arm, and place it above the door, as in *Figure 13—A—2*, but with palm fully opened.
3. Place the palm of the sound arm over that of the sore arm to keep the sore arm in that position as you do the simple movement. Now,
4. Do the Two-Arm Doorway Stretch again, the same as for

broadening the shoulders. But *do not* hold the position at the end of the movement.

Benefits of the Two-Arm Doorway Stretch for your shoulder-joint

By stretching the ligaments and tendons of your sore shoulder, you improve the circulation to the joint. That removes the accumulated waste products in the joint space faster and keeps the joint lubricated. That reduces the size of the engorged bursa and eases the pain. You are then able to move the arm to a greater range and that, in turn, improves the circulation still more and reduces the inflammation within the joint, and consequently the pain reduces still more, too. The pathway to recovery has been thrown wide open.

Frequency

Do it 10 times in the morning, and 10 times at night, until the condition vanishes. And it will do so much faster than you dream possible.

Case histories

HOW LESTER TONED UP HIS ANTI-GRAVITY MUSCLES, SQUARED AND BROADENED HIS SHOULDERS

Lester was a short man near 30 with a faulty posture that bent his back in an increasingly round arc. He stood or sat all day long at work and used his hands, and for years his shoulders had drooped and narrowed, and his shoulder blades stuck out like wings, and were stiff to move. But he felt no special pain, and diagnosis revealed no clinical symptoms. But Lester no longer felt like his former bouncing, teen-aged self. He felt, instead, like a fainting weakling whenever he stood an average length of time, and his shoulders hung on him like the wings of a dying bird. He suffered from mysterious "hanging pains," too. Yet, he was blindly in love with Lorraine, the fascinating office clerk, who treated him just like any other fellow employee. Lester considered himself to be a poor castoff.

I showed Lester how to tone up his anti-gravity muscles, as well as how to do the Yogi Spread, square and broaden his shoulders, and automatically lessen his wrong-back curve.

To his amazement, his shoulders squared and broadened enough to be noticed, *in a week*, and his "hanging pains" lessened remarkably. For once he felt like somebody again, and regained his confidence in himself.

He made swift progress with Lorraine after that. Lester was swiftly regaining his natural, inborn sex appeal.

How Miles Altered the Universal Misconception of His True Personality

Miles was a modest, mild-mannered young man of 25 who would not hurt a fly. Yet, the opposite sex considered him mercilessly selfish, insufferably conceited, and possessing borderline pugilistic tendencies. Miles was handsome, too, in an attractively masculine manner, and possessed a good physique. Women were drawn to him at sight, but they promptly turned hostile towards him. Miles was in a quandary, for he longed to marry and raise a family. Time and again he tried to alter his personality to please different women he met, but his success with them did not improve.

Miles, I noticed, walked with a slight lean to the right, his right shoulder hanging about 1¼ inches lower than his left, and his right arm swinging noticeably more than his left. His head and neck, in fact, bent towards his lower right shoulder like a boxer getting ready to score a knockout with his right. It presented a confusing contrast to his conscientious, altruistic face. But, tragic to say, it held one's attention more than his face did because it involved a much larger portion of his anatomy. One felt instinctively like preparing to duck the crushing blow that might explode his way every time Miles' right arm swung forward. Miles' legs seemed to follow into the movement, too, as if he were swaggering with his bully-like leaning.

On X-ray, Miles' back was clinically normal, indicating that his faulty posture did not result from a wrong-back curve. His faulty posture was just habitual, and was clinically known as postural lateral curvature. His vertebral bodies and spinal disks, in other words, had not been worn down sideways into wedge shapes. His faulty postural habit, however, had created an undesirable visual impression on the observer and completely misled him about Miles' true character. As a matter of fact, *even after* people knew him and understood his true character, they still changed their minds about him when they saw him standing or moving.

I had Miles do the Yogi Spread to square his shoulders. It stretched the shortened cuff of his right shoulder more than that of his left and started evening them. Since he already owned a chinning bar, I advised him to hang from it, now and then, by the arm of his right (or lower) shoulder, like the Yogi would hang from a tree branch.

I saw Miles a few weeks later. Already he showed a marked change. Not long after that, I was delighted to learn from him that he was "going steady" with the "most charming girl" he had ever met—and that she was the first one who had treated him like he "really was"!

How 55-Year-Old "Old Man" Quentin Remodeled His Time-Disfigured Appearance

Quentin was 55 years old and the father of three, ages 25, 21 and 18. His wife and family were fond of him, but they considered him a "good old man" who should be satisfied to fade away gracefully, now that he was elderly. But, thought Quentin resentfully, he was *only* 55! His reasoning mind was at its best! And, he was even still active sexually!

He refused to accept the "good old man" role. He had worked all his life and had saved to retire in a few more years and enjoy full leisure, at last, with his wife, Ada. Instead, was he then supposed to sit placidly by and await Gabriel's call?

Quentin raged secretly within himself. He had hoped to achieve his goals in life, and then to retire and be admired for what he had accomplished for himself and his family. He wished to be admired, besides, like a man still in his prime!

He stared at himself in the mirror and his breathing faltered. He wasn't much overweight. But, just look at his drooping, narrow shoulders, and at his somewhat bent-over back! He wore an impatient frown, too, and at times felt a vague, dragging aching in his spine. He *did* look like a man who had "thrown away his life for his family," and who had nothing left now, except an aging carcass. He did not resent having given his all for his family, he reflected, but he did resent being relegated to the scrapheap in a hurry! After all, his own life counted, too! His family should consider him as young as possible, so that he could enjoy his golden years with some pride in himself! Instead, they just kept reassuring him not to worry about *after* he was old and feeble. *Old and feeble!*

When Quentin's fears of prostate trouble turned out to be groundless, he confided his secret family resentments to me. I told him to do the Yogi Spread to counteract the distorting strain of faulty posture on his back, shoulders, joints and spinal disks and to regain natural, inborn sex appeal and stop giving the impression that he was a "tired old man."

In less than a month Quentin's shoulders were higher and broader, his back was noticeably straighter, and he rarely felt anymore the vague, dragging, aching pains in his spine. His frown left with it, and he acted jaunty now. His family, too, he confessed, studied him with surprise. His own confidence that he was still sexually attractive and in his prime zoomed, and his whole attitude towards life changed.

Summary of the steps for using the well-guarded Yoga secrets for sex appeal at any age

In order to apply the well-guarded Yoga secrets for sex appeal you have to counteract the battering of the four horsemen of the mastabah on your body. That will bring back optimism, determination and all the other invincible traits of your natural, inborn psychological powers, and restore your sex appeal. You do so by:

1. Toning up your anti-gravity muscles with Yogatone.
2. Lessening your wrong-back curves with Yogametrics and removing the distorting and unflattering picture of your true personality which they present (to women, especially).
3. Counteracting the compressive pushdown of faulty posture on your back, shoulders, joints and spinal disks.
4. Squaring and broadening your shoulders with minimum effort with the Yogi Spread.

The moment you start changing physically with these well-guarded Yoga secrets, your mind fills with confidence, optimism, determination and the other invincible traits of your natural, inborn psychologic powers, and that brings back your lost sex appeal.

Yoga Secrets for Self-Mastery

5

All the outstanding achievements of Yoga are based upon self-mastery. The Yogi spends up to 20 years, either alone in the jungle, or "buried" in a sealed hut with only a small opening at the top, meditating and subjecting himself to the tortures of cruel disciplines and long-maintained unhealthy postures, in order to perfect his power of self-mastery. Self-mastery is the foundation of the unbelievable mental and health benefits of Yoga, but to acquire it without a scientific knowledge of the body is to risk losing more than you gain. These well-guarded Yoga secrets have been carefully studied and scientifically refined for *your own use*, to enable you to gain the utmost from them fast, without subjecting yourself to cruel disciplines and long-maintained unhealthy postures. The case histories at the end prove how effective they can be for you.

How you yourself and the four horsemen of the mastabah deplete your natural inborn power of self-mastery

You yourself and the four horsemen of the mastabah reduce your own natural, inborn power of self-mastery, mainly by:

1. Narrowing your vertebral openings.
2. Letting the larger muscles of your body lose their tone.
3. Letting yourself be ruled by fears.

4. Letting yourself become the slave of bad habits.
5. Letting yourself be ruled by anger.
6. Letting yourself be ruled by maddening worry and anxiety.

You will now be shown how you and those four horsemen bring on these unwanted changes in you and deplete your natural, inborn power of self-mastery, and the refined, scientifically perfected Yoga secrets for counteracting them.

How your narrowed vertebral openings weaken your power of self-mastery

The squeezing of your narrowed vertebral openings on your spinal nerves creates a state of subclinical irritation in your spinal nerves. This eventually provokes in your brain the sensation of an inadequately sent message from your body, and in your body the sensation of an inadequately delivered command from your brain. The squeezing on your spinal nerves, in fact, actually changes the very messages of truth and commands themselves, in the following ways:

1. The squeezing tends to slow down the time your spinal nerves wait before starting to transmit the messages they send from your body to your brain, and the commands they deliver from your brain to your body.
2. The squeezing modifies the speed and intensity of the transmission of the message or command and thereby *alters the nature of the sensation itself* so that, actually, a *different* message or command is sent to your brain or body.
3. The squeezing slows down the speed of recovery of the spinal nerve from the effort of transmitting.

The whole nerve timing, consequently, is off, and there is a leak of nerve energy in your spinal nerves. The commanded muscle or gland, therefore, contracts, or relaxes, or secretes more *slowly* than it was commanded to by your brain. Also destroyed is the isochronism (the uniform timing) of the response of your brain to the message sent to it by your body. Your power of self-mastery is then obviously limited, for both your brain and your body have lost a certain degree of absolutely necessary, natural, inborn control over each other. In order to regain as much as possible of your lost natural, inborn self-mastery then, you have to widen your narrowed vertebral openings as much as possible. You will be taught how to do so now.

The Vertodiv: the Yogametric simple movement to widen your narrowed vertebral openings as much as possible

The secret simple movement for widening your vertebral openings as much as possible, safely, is the Vertodiv (*Figure 14*).

Figure 14

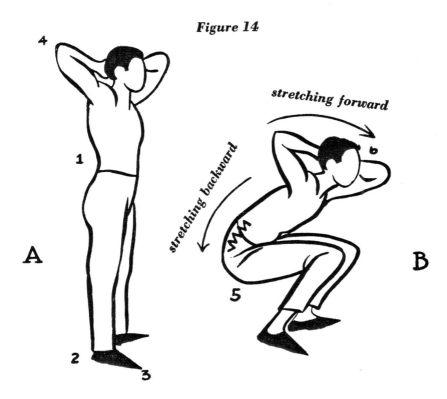

The position to assume (Figure 14—A)

1. Stand normally straight, with
2. Your heels about a foot apart, and with
3. Your toes pointing outwards at about 45 degree angles.
4. Place your hands on the back of your head and lock them by folding their fingers into each other.

How to do this simple movement (Figure 14—B)

5. Squat now and
6. Draw your head forwards with your hands, *gently*
7. Hold the position for two seconds, and then
8. Stand and drop your hands by your sides.

What the Vertodiv does for you

1. The Vertodiv stretches your back in the the safe, forward-enough position. It does not require you to bend backwards and injure yourself. (You will be shown these dangers later.) Nor does it require you to bend acutely forwards against locked hips and also risk injuring yourself.
2. The Vertodiv stretches your back to the full limit, safely, too, because it pulls it out from two directions. The down-pull of your hips in the squat, stretches the lower half of your spine. The forward pull of your hands behind your head, at the very same time, stretches the upper half of your spine, as well as your neck. *But pull it gently.*
3. The contracted position of your abdomen also draws it in and flattens it.

Frequency

Twice every morning.

The Yoga secret of Macro-Muscle-Tone for filling you instantly, at any time, with your full, natural, inborn power of self-mastery

After your spinal disks have shrunken to a decisive degree with the passage of years, it is impossible for you to regain permanently your natural, inborn power of self-mastery because you cannot again widen your narrowed vertebral openings permanently to their original diameters and regain permanently your full, natural, inborn Spino-Volt. You *can* regain your natural, inborn power of self-mastery completely, though temporarily, as the Yogis do, with a secretly created psychologic power, and control others against their wills. That well-guarded, secretly created psychologic power is Yoga Macro-Muscle-Tone.

Yoga Macro-Muscle-Tone is an incomparable discovery also for increasing your self-mastery tremendously any time during the day when you combat a bad habit, face a new situation, or force yourself to study or engage in any other necessary but unwelcome task. You can, for that reason, use and make extraordinary gains with it *at once* before you even widen your narrowed vertebral openings.

The Yogis happened to discover their extremely well-guarded secret of Macro-Muscle-Tone because, in their supersensitive concern with the inner sensations of their bodies, they found, during their torturous disciplines, that self-mastery was intimately related to memory of muscular effort. If your mind, for instance, harbors only ideas of a flabby body *without* solid muscles, your character will be altered by that intimate memory. Your own character, in other words, will then become flabby, due to the "psychologic reflex" which the sensations of anatomical flabbiness flash into your conscious and subconscious minds. You will, as a result, feel as frustrated and powerless as the man who tries to halt his car suddenly, but with the dreaded realization that his brakes won't hold. *Even when you know* how to meet every situation in life, to put it another way, you will lack the fiber to do it. Thus, you acquire anxieties, feelings of inferiority, undue shyness and a general attitude of easy and total discouragement in anything you undertake. You might end up taking stimulants to provide you with the backbone you lack.

The best stimulant you can take to give you that backbone, though, is to add tone to your larger muscles, or Yoga Macro-Muscle-Tone. Adding tone suddenly to your larger muscles fills your conscious and subconscious minds with a broad, masculine sense of well-being and surplus energy. Toning your *smaller* muscles, in contrast, only fills your minds with a narrow, feminine sense of petty immediacy and personal inadequacy. That's why the Yogis perfected their well-guarded secret of Yoga Macro-Muscle-Tone. You will be taught that miraculous secret right now, as well as the most effective muscles to tone up for it.

The secret macro-muscles to tone up to regain your lost, natural, inborn power of self-mastery

The Yogis, due to the thousands of years of masters behind them, discovered the larger (macro) muscles to tone up to regain fastest and strongest their lost, natural, inborn power of self-mastery.

The secret macro-muscles of your body are the big muscles of your shoulders, the big muscles of the back of your neck, of your chest, your triceps, at the back of your hips, of the fronts and sides of your thighs, and of the backs of your calves. In clinical examinations of fearful, suppressed persons, these muscles are usually found to be flabby and tone-less. Their smaller muscles, in contrast, tend to be abnormally contracted. The lifetimes of traumatic fear experiences of such people, intensified by the dominations of others over them, force them to "cross their fingers and bear up" under them. The resulting feelings of frustration, coupled with the helpless inabilities to act and end those situations, subconsciously contract the smaller muscles of such people rather than their larger ones. Those smaller muscles are: the deeper muscle layers of your back (or the muscles which are directly attached between your individual vertebrae); the muscles of the front of your neck (including those of your voice); and the muscles of your face, hands, fingers and feet. That's why when you are fearful, your back tends to be stiff, you tend to stutter and stammer, your cheek tends to quiver, your hands to fidget, and your feet to be restless. It is the reason why the noted osteopath, Dr. Louisa Burns, wrote that, "the person who needs bolstering up should be compelled to use his large muscles," and regularly so in order to erase from his conscious and subconscious minds the ingrained memory of his flabby body, for this memory is intimately associated with his life failures. He should replace it with a memory of toned-up large muscles, for *this* memory is intimately associated with a feeling of body domination which *will* bolster up the person.

Dr. Burns had scratched the surface, but Yoga had dug right down through it and ripped open the secret. Yoga had found, in crude fashion, that your larger (macro) muscles cover a larger area of your body than your other bulky muscles and perform your greatest muscle feats. With the muscles of your shoulders, back, chest and triceps, you lift, push and hit. With those of your hips, thighs and calves, you walk, run, leap, climb—or raise your body off the ground. Your smaller muscles, however, primarily aid your larger (macro) muscles because with them you breathe, speak, hold, turn, direct. The specific macro-muscles mentioned, too, are *the* ones for you to tone up. They _extend_ (straighten) your big joints, and are therefore the ones which bring you the strongest rule over your body, and consequently spark in you the strongest feeling of mental domination. This is true because they are the muscles that push you forwards when you walk or run; push you upwards when you jump or climb; push the weight away from you when you press it; pitch the ball when you throw; swing the bat; hurl your fist out when you hit. Your other macro-muscles are *flexor* muscles.

These are your biceps, your abdominal muscles, the muscles at the backs of your thighs. These macro-muscles *draw* objects or weights *towards* you, or bend your body towards *itself* (your abdominal muscles). Measured by weight-lifting standards, these flexor macro-muscles possess *far less* power than your extensor macro-muscles.

Your conscious and subconscious minds, therefore, come to expect power and domination from your *extensor* macro-muscles. For, when you bend your body towards you (as you do with your abdominal muscles), it is like bowing to authority and suggests humility and servility to your conscious mind. But when you push something up and away from you, it is like becoming taller, reaching for the stars and assuming full equality with, or unchallengeable authority over, others. Toning-up your extensor macro-muscles, then, as the Yogis secretly found, is the incomparable quick shortcut for filling yourself *instantly, any time,* with lost, natural, inborn power of self-mastery.

NOTE: Technically speaking, the muscles of the backs of your calves are *flexor* muscles. But since they lift your body off the ground when you walk, run or jump, their psychological effect on your conscious mind is similar to that of your extensor muscles. That's why the Yogis wisely added them to the most effective, extensor Macro-Muscle-Tone group.

How to protect yourself against being selfishly dominated by others

An important reason for your acquiring self-mastery is to enable you to control yourself at will, so that you can prevent others from dominating you. That amounts to your greatest social and business gain from self-mastery. And it is a most practical application of Yoga Macro-Muscle-Tone. You will, therefore, be taught how to use it to banish fear instantly, how to control anger instantly, and how to be cool-headed, calm, or commercially practical-minded, instantly, no matter how heated the situation may become.

But, first of all, you have to learn the well-guarded technique of Yoga Macro-Muscle-Tone. The technique is not only unbelievably simple and brief to apply, but you require *no huge muscles nor unusual strength* for it either! The softer your macro-muscles are, in fact, the easier you can tone them up and fill your mind with the confidence, optimism and fearlessness that bring you a feeling of mental domination over your body, and therefore, suggestively, of *over the other person*, too.

Why? Because a brief, effortless contraction of that soft macro-muscle will feel abnormally strong to *your* mind, and that will psychologically imbue it with a consciousness of super self-mastery and mental domination over your body, and over other people. From the health standpoint, of course, it is wiser for you to possess stronger and harder muscles. From the standpoint alone of filling you with a conviction of unconquerable mental domination and self-mastery, though, all that counts is how your mind reacts to your macro-muscle contraction, and therefore how it enables you to banish fear instantly. So, study and apply right away in your daily life, the Myo-Pector, the Yoga secret for banishing fear instantly.

How to banish fear instantly with the Myo-Pector

1. Sit relaxed before your mirror, with your torso naked, in order to see exactly what you are doing.
2. Rest your hands, palms *down*, on your thighs, with the tips of your middle finger about two inches back from your knees.
3. Now, lower your shoulders forcibly towards the ground. That places your chest muscles into their best angles of pull, because you have rotated your humerus (the bone of your upper arm) at the shoulder joint, where your chest muscles insert.

4. Next, move your shoulders inwards fast, towards each other, as far as they will go (about one-half inch), and tense your chest hard at the same time.

5. Hold the contraction for two seconds. Then relax. You swiftly acquire the unconquerable feeling of a solid musculature breastplate.

That is how to myo-tense your chest muscles and banish fear instantly any time it assails or overtakes you, and thereby protect yourself against being selfishly dominated by others.

How to control your anger instantly with Yoga Macro-Muscle-Tone

Jim, who may be a fellow worker, an associate, a romantic rival, or even your boss, has done something reprehensible to you behind your back, and it has made you furious. Jim had no justifiable reason for doing it either. Perhaps he hoped to hurt your chances of advancement, or envied how well you got along with others, or tried to poison against you the girl you both admire. You are so angry you want to destroy him.

When in such a mood, many a man has committed murder, and has spent the rest of his life regretting it. Even if you explode at Jim only with words, you might merely make a spectacle of yourself.

There is *one thing* you must do at once, before all is lost. You must control your anger instantly. *Then* you can think clearly and meet the situation squarely.

Control your anger instantly by Yoga Macro-Muscle-Toning your triceps muscles alone. This is how you do it. Stand or sit at ease, with your arms hanging limply at your sides. Now—smile at what you have heard, particularly for your informant or accuser to see, should he be present. Keep your arms in the same position meanwhile, but *subtly straighten* them by moving your forearms backwards about two inches, and slightly outwards.

You will experience a sudden, gripping contraction in the backs of your upper arms. Maintain it for two seconds. Then relax your arms.

Blood will flush most of your upper arms, for your triceps constitute about two-thirds of their mass. You will *feel* as if you have just leaped at your defamer and beaten him. Your dangerous anger vanishes at once, and your conscious mind can think clearly again and meet the situation squarely and conquer it.

How to relieve a maddening worry and anxiety instantly with Yoga Macro-Muscle-Tone

A disheartening prospect awaits you just ahead, such as a decisive examination, a court trial, the battle line, a perilous business move, or something which could make or break you. You yearn to get out of it, but have no choice. It may even be the big opportunity you have long awaited. You can hardly eat, sleep, talk, think, do your work, or relax. Your family, friends or associates try to reassure you, but you still keep worrying about it. You actually feel faint at times, as if your heart has skipped a few beats. You will be a nervous wreck by the time you have to meet the situation.

There is *one thing* you have to do repeatedly between now and that decisive day. You have to stop your maddening worry and anxiety *instantly* every time it seizes you. *Then* you can save your mental energy for the situation itself.

Relieve your maddening worry and anxiety instantly, every time it seizes you, by Yoga Macro-Muscle-Toning the backs of your calves, the fronts of your thighs and the backs of your hips. This is how you do it. Every time the maddening worry and anxiety seizes you, go up on your toes (if you are seated, stand up) and tense the whole length of your legs, from your hips to the soles of your feet, as hard as you can. You will experience a sudden, pillar-like contraction on the backs of your calves, on the fronts of your thighs, and in the backs of your hips, as if you were about to leap into the air and shake off all your troubles in a flash.

Maintain the contraction for two seconds. Then stand solidly on your feet again.

If you are lying down, resting on your back, you may Macro-Muscle-Tone those muscles by pointing footwards hard with your toes for two seconds. For the best effect, though, do the simple movement standing up.

The about-to-leap-into-the-air and-shake-off-your-troubles-in-a-flash feeling will, reflexly, fill your conscious mind with that very suggestion, and your conscious mind will instantly throw off your maddening worry and anxiety. Shake it off the same way each time it seizes you, and it will practically disappear altogether and let you save your energy for the actual situation.

How to control any bad habit instantly with the Yogatone Exhaler

The mastery of Yoga requires such strict discipline that no bad habit can be allowed to predominate over it. The Yogi is therefore an incomparable master of controlling bad habits. His austerity in that direction, in fact, is too well known to require further comment. But his method of controlling bad habits is swift and decisive because he has so many superhuman goals ahead for his mind and body to reach, that he cannot waste time tolerating such "insignificant obstacles" as bad habits. And yet, he, too, is plagued with bad habits. The Yogis have, consequently, secretly devised a successful move to control any bad habit instantly—the Yogatone Exhaler. Learn how to do it at once, for it is very simple. But it will knock out any bad habit in you any time, and every time you do it you achieve increased mastery over the habit. Following is how you do it.

You are bothered incessantly by a bad habit that is either ruining your life, or which could ruin it in time . . . a bad habit like excessive smoking or drinking, unfounded suspicion of your wife or business associates, or an abnormal relish for unhealthy foods, etc. Repeatedly, you have tried to control it, but you invariably give in to it. You are disgusted with yourself afterwards and vow never again to submit to it Next time, though, you submit to it again.

The next time the bad habit tempts you, exhale at once. Keep on exhaling until you empty your lungs so thoroughly that you feel as if your stomach is touching your back. Then, for one second, contract your abdomen as tightly as you can.

Immediately relax and let your lungs fill up naturally again.

That's all you have to do. Repeat the Yogatone Exhaler if the temptation for the bad habit still lingers on for the moment. But you probably won't have to.

The Yogatone Exhaler works so miraculously because, when you exhale thoroughly and then contract your abdominal muscles tightly, you practically "empty" the air from your lungs. (Your lungs, of course, are *never* completely emptied of air while you are alive). So, you suddenly feel like a drowning man when he is being asphyxiated by the water. Your sympathetic nervous system (your fighting nerves) at once rushes to your rescue in a frantic, savage manner—or in a much more savage manner than it does when you just hold your breath too long. This frantic, savage manner flashes itself reflexly to your conscious mind and kindles a subconscious fury in you that casts out the bad habit. Do so every time the bad habit grips you, and you will never again be its slave.

Case histories

HOW BRUCE BROKE THE "PERPETUAL EATING" HABIT THAT WAS WRECKING HIS DIGESTION AND FATTENING HIM FAST

Bruce was plagued with the bad habit of eating repeatedly between meals. During every "break" at work he gobbled down some cake, pie, ice cream, a banana split, malted milk, custard, a chocolate bar or something of the kind.

"I have to!" he pleaded with me. "I feel hungry between meals! I'd be weak without a full feeling under my belt!" But now he suffered with an acid stomach, belching, heartburn, crawling sensations on his face and scalp, headaches, and bloated belly. He had lost energy and ambition, was restless and wanted only to sit and eat all day. His weight and blood pressure were gaining, too.

I told him that he was digging his own grave with his teeth. I even showed him that his blood sugar was bordering on diabetes. He was alarmed and swore to limit his daily meals to three and to eliminate the sweets.

Bruce returned in a month—*in worse condition than ever*. He could *not* control his eating habits, he said. The moment he saw or thought of food, or felt the least bit hungry after a meal, he'd go crazy unless he put something in his stomach. He offered to compromise by taking only light beverages, like fruit juices, between meals. But I directed him to imbibe only water between meals, as the healthiest Yogis did. He had to allow his hyper-secreting digestive glands, I explained to him, to rest completely between meals and atrophy (or shrink) back to normal and decrease his stomach acidity.

When Bruce failed to follow those directions strictly, I taught him the Yogatone Exhaler and directed him to use it every time he felt hungry between meals, and instead to drink *only* plain water. He phoned me excitedly within ten days and reported unbelievable progress. When I saw him at the end of the month, he looked like a different person. His waist was noticeably flatter, the belching and fullness of his stomach had practically vanished, and his digestion headaches had gone. His blood pressure was also falling satisfactorily, his urine sugar had dropped decidedly, and he had lost fifteen pounds. He was able to think about and even see food between meals, without getting over-excited about it. With the Yogatone Exhaler, impulsive-eating Bruce had broken the "perpetual eating" habit that was wrecking his digestion and making him prone to diabetes.

How Restless Larry Adapted Himself to Reading as a Hobby, and Derives a Steady Stream of Lucrative, Original Ideas

Larry had developed into a restless, dissatisfied person who leaped superficially from one subject of interest to another. The habit had not only handicapped him severely in school, but also had held him back in his career because he was too scatterbrained to tackle anything that he could not solve in short order. Time and again he tried to absorb himself in subject after subject, but he was impatient with their technical details.

Larry had obviously lost his natural, inborn power of self-mastery and was now tragically lacking in self-discipline. During his visit I noticed that he habitually held and fumbled objects with his fingers (his small muscles). But when I asked him if he enjoyed systematic exercise, he replied with a definite "no!" His memories of muscular effort, in other words, were almost exclusively those of his small muscles (the petty, feminine-like muscles whose predominant use produced a feeling of inefficiency and lack of power). This diagnosis was confirmed when he stripped and I observed how stiff his spine was from the spasm-contractions of his deepest back muscles (his small, intervertebral muscles). His restless features and feet confirmed those symptoms.

I taught Larry how to apply Yoga Macro-Muscle-Tone to his large extensor muscles whenever he felt restless, especially to those of his back and triceps, and then to resume his concentration.

Five months later, he contacted me and confessed that he had changed so thoroughly not long after applying Yoga Macro-Muscle-Tone that for some time now he had been reading deep, technical material as a hobby. What's more, he had extracted from the seemingly minor details in it, such a stream of original ideas that his company had made use of a number of them and had found them so profitable that it had rewarded him with a handsome raise and an attractive promotion.

Summary of the steps for using Yoga for self-mastery

In order to apply Yoga for self-mastery, you have to counteract the battering of the four horsemen of the mastabah on your body, as well as overcome the impulsive control of your mind over your body. In that way you preserve a considerable part of your natural, inborn power of self-mastery and save it from unnecessary depletion. That automatically exerts a psychological impact on your mind which fills you with confidence, optimism, determination, and with all the other invincible qualities of the natural, inborn psychological powers of your mind over your body, instead of your body over your mind. You simply do so by:

1. Widening your vertebral openings to increase your Spino-Volt.
2. Regaining the tone of the larger muscles of your body with Yoga Macro-Muscle-Tone.
3. Banishing your fears instantly with Yoga Macro-Muscle-Tone.
4. Controlling your anger instantly with Yoga Macro-Muscle-Tone.
5. Relieving your maddening worries and anxieties instantly with Yoga Macro-Muscle-Tone.
6. Controlling your bad habits instantly with the Yogatone Exhaler.

The moment you apply these Yoga powers your mind feels relieved and you acquire mental domination over yourself. The resulting psychological impact brings back your natural, inborn power of self-mastery, free of fears.

How to Use Yoga to Get What You Want

6

The nucleus of all Yoga achievement is the astounding power of concentration into which the Yogi can place his mind. With it he can master new subjects with baffling speed, make his mind so oblivious to his surroundings that nothing in them can disturb him, capture and enslave the interests of others in him at the snap of a finger, and make himself so mentally alert that he can detect the cleverest schemes and the slickest tricks of others against him (as *you wish* you could in business, romance, or domestic life, for example) before the culprits can victimize him with them. And he can do so *at any age*. His well-guarded secrets of concentration have been carefully studied and refined for *your own use* in the practical Western world to enable you to make the utmost gains from them fast, without banishing yourself to long, solitary sessions, or subjecting your body to insufferable self-castigations. The case histories prove how effective they can be for bringing you unsurpassable powers of concentration safely and with unbelievable speed.

How the four horsemen of the mastabah reduce your natural, inborn power of concentration

The four horsemen of the mastabah reduce your natural, inborn power of concentration by:

1. Weakening it all through your life by accelerating the normal wearing down of your lumbosacral joint.
2. Bringing on, as a consequence, subclinical (and later, clinical, or felt) low-back pain, like sciatic pains.
3. Narrowing the vertebral openings of your lumbosacral joint and therefore diminishing your natural, inborn mental alertness.

You will now be shown how the four horsemen bring about these unwanted changes in you and reduce your natural, inborn power of concentration, and the refined, scientifically perfected Yoga secrets for counteracting them.

The direct causes of low-back sciatic pains in man

The direct causes of low-back sciatic pains in man are severe trauma (physical injuries). These are due mainly to the twisting injuries common to football, soccer or skiing; to excessive hopping, skipping and sudden changes in direction in such sports as basketball, volleyball, tennis, skipping rope, competitive walking, long distance running, broad jumping, ground acrobatics, and so forth. Crushing injuries, in other words, *do not* cause low-back sciatic pains; such pains are caused, rather, by the mild, but oft-repeated, stress and strain of such sports as mentioned. The total effects of their mild repetitions, however, accumulate in time and *equal* that of the sudden, severe injury. *Severe* continued trauma, though, affects the plumber, the piano mover, the street driller, the miner, the blacksmith.

Every movement of a joint causes a trauma in that joint because the bones comprising the joint then rub against each other through the thin synovial membrane and its fluid, which separate them. That's why the bones comprising the joint wear down each other in time. If the trauma is stopped and the blood circulation to the joint is maintained (by widening the narrowed vertebral opening that squeezes the sympathetic nerve that supplies its blood vessels), the effects of the trauma on the joint are repaired swiftly. But if the blood circulation to the joint is slowed down (as it is when the vertebral opening squeezes the nerve that controls its blood vessels), the effects of the trauma on the joint are not repaired, and *arthritis begins to form.*

Those multiple, mild injuries, called "the microtraumatic" injuries by the noted orthopedist Lewin, are, then, the direct causes of low-back sciatic pains in man, even when they are still sub-clinical and therefore still not felt by the consciousness. Not only that, but since they are brought about by the four horsemen of the mastabah, you *cannot* avoid them. Every day, for that reason, you subject your joints (and, particularly, your lumbosacral joint, located at the base of your spine) to an amazing amount of multiple, mild injuries in such common, unsuspected activities as gardening, swimming, golf, even in "heel walking," which is the way most people walk. With high heels, women subject themselves to an incredible amount of microtraumatic injury. They jar their spines, with each step, all the way up to their heads. Thus, they "rattle" their vertebrae together and wear down the porotic cylindrical bodies, and thin their spinal disks. Their narrowed vertebral bodies, as a result, narrow more and more. Everybody is subjected to microtraumatic injury even in the daily twists and bumps of regular life, or in doing simple things in awkward positions. Everybody's subconscious mind, as a consequence, is constantly subject to an increasing stream of messages of nerve irritation from his increasingly hard squeezed spinal nerves . . . and especially from the spinal nerve of his lumbosacral joint, which registers sciatic pain, either felt or unfelt (either clinical or subclinical). In either case, such a pain significantly reduces your natural, inborn power of concentration.

How low-back pain results from the greatly accelerated wearing down of your lumbosacral joint

As man evolved from the four-footed to the two-footed position, abnormal stresses and strains developed on his spine. Over a period of time, such as the normal process of aging, these stresses and strains cause degenerative changes (in general, a wearing down) in the different vertebral joints of the spine. And, degenerative changes are responsible for most of mankind's aches and pains: both due to the *sub*clinical ones of which he is only subconsciously aware, and due to the *clinical* ones of which he *is* consciously aware.

Your lumbosacral joint, though, which is located at the base of your spine (*Figure 15*) wears down earlier and to a greater extent than the other joints of your spine. That's because your fifth

Figure 15

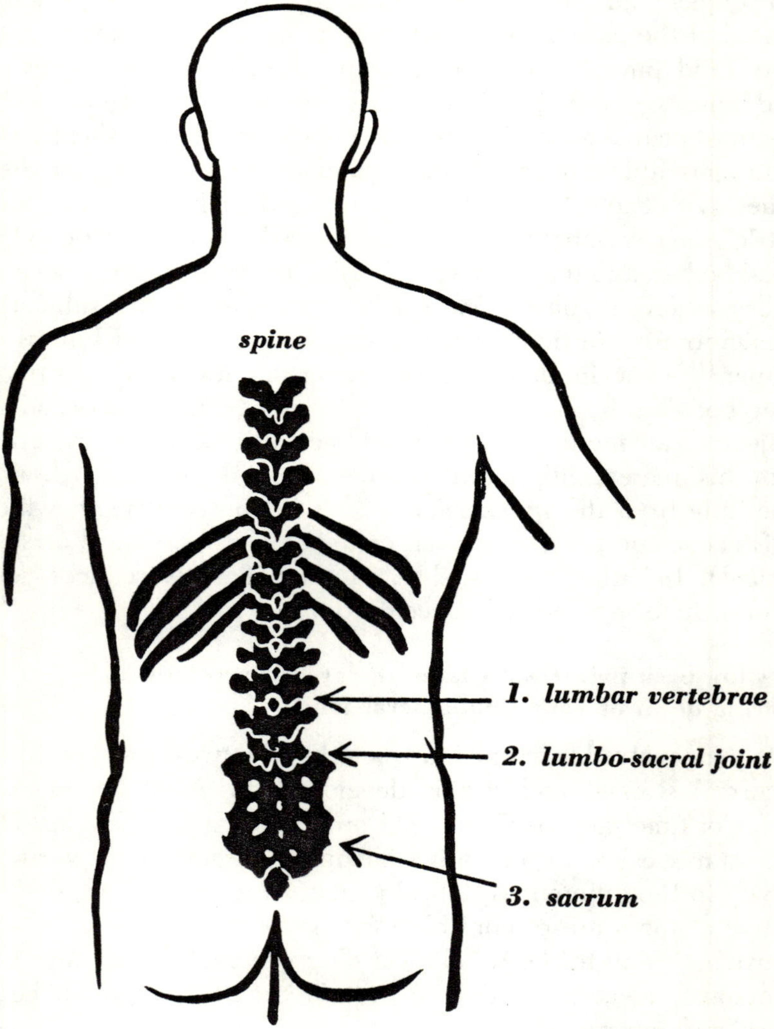

spine

1. *lumbar vertebrae*

2. *lumbo-sacral joint*

3. *sacrum*

lumbar vertebra (the last vertebra, at the bottom of your spine) forms the top half of your lumbosacral joint and differs from all the other vertebra in its function.

As the end-link of the flexible chain of your spinal column, it is the most important shock absorber of your whole spine because it must absorb most of the shock on it. Your lumbosacral joint thus starts wearing down very early in your life, or as soon as you assume the sitting posture and stand your vertebrae one on top of another, plus the weight of your head on them. Not much later, when you stumble around trying to walk, the jarring of ground resistance adds to the traumas of the four horsemen of the mastabah on your vertebral joints and wears them down still faster. Bending, or twisting, your spine down towards the ground, adds still more to the constant wear-and-tear of these traumas on your vertebral joints, and so the resulting wearing down of your vertebral joints increases with time, that is, with your age. Since 50 per cent or more of the movement of your trunk below your torso occurs at your lumbosacral region, this joint wears down much faster than your other joints.

The four, long, slender ligaments which hold this structurally weak joint together, besides, can fail to support it *any time* the protecting muscles around it relax too much, *even for a moment.* This can happen, for instance, any time you contract the muscles of your lower back hard and suddenly lift a weight, or when you suddenly burst into a sprint to catch a bus or train, or when you engage in any action, or assume any position in which your body is all at once thrown into a flexed or twisted attitude. It will even happen if you abruptly *try* to bend forward when your lower back muscles are tight. In fact, *every time* you make a move, such as every time you walk, run, climb stairs, sit and turn, lie down, get up, carry anything, and so on, the muscles protecting your lumbosacral joint *do* relax too much and leave it at the mercy of its four, long, slender ligaments. This constant, repeated relaxation of the muscles of that joint all day long, made still more dangerous by the incessant pounding of the four horsemen of the mastabah on the joint's structure, eventually leads to postural and chronic strain, because ligaments *do not* withstand repeated or continuous strain as well as muscles do.

As long as your muscles and ligaments, however, possess enough strength and tone to enable you to continue your activities without fatigue, you will suffer no symptoms from the incessant trauma. Your lumbosacral joint is then said to be "compensated." When its muscles weaken from lack of tone, though, and its ligaments weaken from strain, low-back pain results.

How your steadily degenerating lumbosacral joint brings on sciatic pain

The lumbosacral joint is inherently weak in the first place, because the spine, which was developed for four-footed function, has been bent *backwards* to accommodate to the right-angle standing position, and to balance itself in it! This new position abnormally widened the lumbosacral joint in front (*Figures 16, 17*) and left it as unstable as that of a dog suddenly walking on its hind-legs. That weakened it and subjected its ligaments and muscles, which now tried to balance it in the upright position, to undue strain. Instead of just fitting within the spinal column like any other vertebral joint, the lumbosacral joint now had to *balance itself* against the inimical forces of the four horsemen of the mastabah (that is, of gravity, faulty posture, weight-bearing, and ground resistance from below). Now, in fact, as the whole body struggled desperately, in its new position, to counterbalance the toppling downpull of gravity and remain upright, the top half of

Figure 16

THE FOUR-LEGGED POSITION

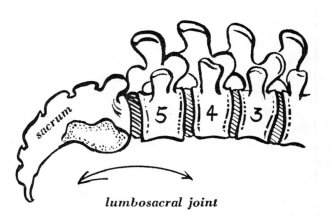

lumbosacral joint

Figure 17

THE UPRIGHT POSITION

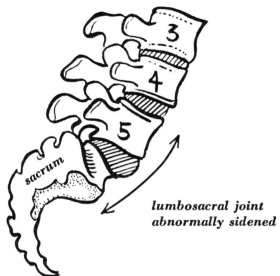

lumbosacral joint
abnormally sidened

Figure 18

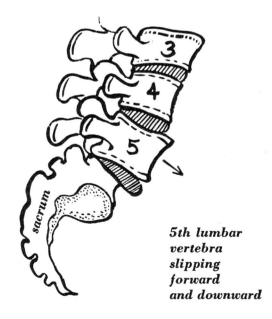

5th lumbar
vertebra
slipping
forward
and downward

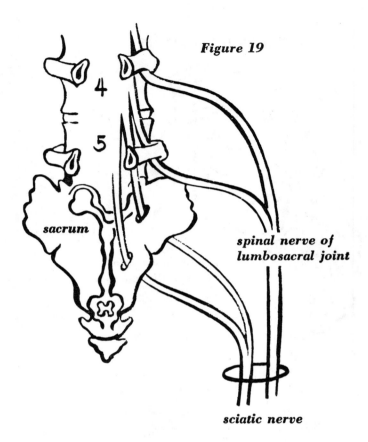

Figure 19

sacrum

*spinal nerve of
lumbosacral joint*

sciatic nerve

the lumbosacral joint was compelled to bear the whole weight of the head and torso. Its lower half, too, was now no longer practically stationary, as it had been in the four-footed position. Now, instead, it was twisted, at different times, forwards, backwards, left or right, in accordance with the body's wobbling efforts to stay upright.

With the ligaments of your lumbosacral joints stretched abnormally by these new, inimical forces, your precariously slanted fifth lumbar vertebra, which forms the upper half of your lumbosacral joint (*Figure 18*), is displaced slightly (but steadily and increasingly, over the years) forwards and downwards, by the downpull of gravity and by the thinning of the spinal disk of the joint. This forward and downward dropping of that vertebra is further encouraged by the fact that the cylindrical body of that particular vertebra is *thicker in front* than it is behind (*Figure 18*). When it starts slipping forwards and downwards, then, it has nothing behind to anchor it back into place, and so it continues to slip farther forwards and downwards with time, as your lumbosacral joint wears down, and pain results.

What occurs then? *Sciatic pain,* because that spinal nerve is an important component of your sciatic nerve (*Figure 19*).

How sciatic pain, even if unfelt, seriously reduces your natural, inborn power of concentration

The inevitable sciatic pain may begin in your leg. You might even experience *no pain,* though, or only a slight pain or discomfort in your lower back. Indeed, for years before you feel sciatic pain (if you ever do) you will be suffering from *subliminal* sciatic pain—or a sciatic pain felt only by your *subconscious* mind. Whether you feel it or not, though, the pain does exist, and it may be constant or spasmodic. It is exaggerated by movement, coughing and sneezing, or by your assuming certain positions. Its unperceived intensity varies from mild to severe, with periods of acute bouts of subclinical pain which may suddenly be perceptible consciously as slight low-back pains. You complain of them, or are even diagnosed, but nothing worth mentioning is found. You are suspected of being a hypochondriac, and so you try to ignore the pain or take pain relievers. *But the pain does exist— subliminally (just below the threshold of your consciousness)—for the chronic strain on the joint is continuing.* It is an *un*-diagnosable pain: an aching and soreness induced or aggravated by movement of your back. You are particularly aware of it when you sneeze, rise after sitting, or get out of bed. You sigh and attribute it to growing old.

The pain has not yet exploded in a crippling lumbago attack, nor has it spread noticeably along your sciatic nerve down your leg to your foot. And it might never be acute enough to send you looking for professional help. All the while, nonetheless, this sly, abusive, "unfelt" pain and soreness flashes its nagging messages to your subconscious mind. Your subconscious mind, in turn, relays it to your conscious mind in the form of mystifying discomforts, pessimistic compulsions about everything, and uncontrollable impatience against sitting and concentrating long on any subject.

This tenderness could be undermining your natural, inborn power of concentration, too, without even suspecting it, and misleading you into assuming that you suffer also from stomach trouble, chronic indigestion and incipient ulcers. This chain of troubles would end if you reassumed the four-footed position in your everyday life; but in the society you live in, that is impractical. So, you grow worse as you continue the hopeless battle against the four horsemen of the mastabah, endure more subliminal pain, and lose more of your natural, inborn power of concentration. Your whole mental machinery is *unsuspectingly disturbed*, but you are aware only that you experience increasing difficulty in mastering new knowledge; in making yourself oblivious enough to your surroundings so nothing can disturb you; in capturing the interests of others; in making yourself so mentally calm that you can detect and abort the cleverest schemes and the slickest tricks of others. You feel frustrated and want desperately to change your environment, your friends, your career—everything about you. Life has come to mean to you only endless dissatisfaction and raging disgust.

The Yogis found the swift, effective way to counteract these physical, and their resulting mental, plagues.

How to master new subjects with the Yogatone Replacer

You are seated in your room with new material to learn or understand for your job; or for advanced study, business use, profitable investment, or for anything whatever. You stare at it and read it, but it makes no sense. Either it is written too technically or ponderously, or your mind just wanders away from it habitually and dwells instead on pleasurable matters. Yet, the material before you could gain you a good promotion, enable you to pass an important examination, open up for you a far more lucrative business prospect, or reveal to you what to be aware of so that you can step wisely into a big new field and maybe get rich. Every time you try to concentrate on the dry new material, though, your mind withdraws from it in utter despair and flees back to your effortless pleasurable thoughts or daydreams. And yet, you have to act *wisely* on the material before it is too late, or before others act on it and leave you out in the cold.

You might, or might not, experience a vague discomfort in your lower back, or even in your hips, as if they are tired of sitting. You are impelled to get up frequently and walk around and do something entirely different—perhaps even to go out and be sociable, or to watch TV. Your lumbosacral joint, in other words, is flashing irritating messages to your subconscious mind; and your subconscious mind, as a result, is reflexly delivering commands to your skeletal muscles to escape from the irritation by moving you around, or by convincing you to do something entirely different, to "work it off" your mind.

You can suppress the continuous irritant with the Yogatone Replacer (*Figures* 20–22).

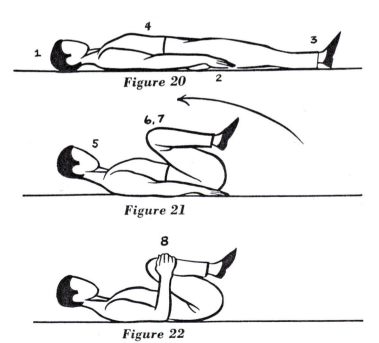

Figure 20

Figure 21

Figure 22

The Yogatone Replacer

The position to assume (Figure 20).

1. Lie flat on your back,
2. Hands holding on to the sides of the bed,
3. Legs straight down.
4. Inhale.

How to do this simple movement (Figures 21, 22).

5. Exhale, and at the same time
6. Bend your knees and
7. Draw both bent legs, *pressed tightly together*, up to your chest. *Remember:* Keep both legs, particularly the knees, *tightly together.*
8. Raise your body off the bed as much as possible, to help bring your chest and knees together. Assure yourself of that by, additionally, hugging your knees to your chest with your arms. (*Figure 22*).
9. Hold for two seconds. Then relax.

What the Yogatone Replacer does for you

1. Develops fine rectus muscles on the front of your abdomen.
2. Wears off the fat there fast.
3. Tremendous aid to uncomplicated constipation if done immediately after arising in the morning and drinking first, a glass and a half of warm water.
4. Most important, right now, it widens your lumbosacral joint and suppresses the continuous irritant.

Frequency

Do it 2–5 times in the morning for the first month; after that, 2 times a day.

How to grow mentally calm swiftly with the Yogatone Tranquilizer

HOW TO DO THE YOGATONE TRANQUILIZER

1. Sit on a chair and hold arms straight out at the sides, at 45 degree angles forward from the shoulders.

Figure 23

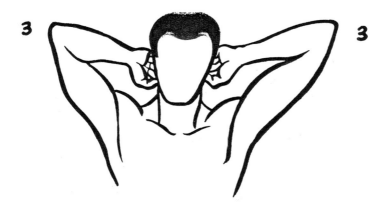

Figure 24

Figure 25

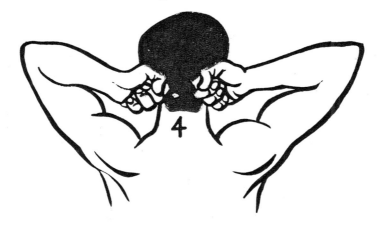

2. Close your fists and flex your arms until your fists stop behind your head (*Figure 24*).
3. Your elbows should now be high and inwards (*Figure 23*).
4. Turn your palms backwards by raising the thumb-halves of your hands BACKWARDS and UPWARDS (*Figure 25*).
5. Now, contract hard, and hold for one second.
6. Relax.

The Yogatone Tranquilizer calms you speedily because, the moment you finish doing it, you feel as if you have just completed a crushing task, or just recovered from an incapacitating illness. Just do it once whenever you are losing your mental calm about anything. If you are not alone at the time, just pretend to be "stretching your bones."

Case histories

How Middle-Aged Bill Made Up, with Surprisingly Little Trouble, the School Credits He Needed for Job Advancement

In order to attain the post he desired in his company, Bill needed more formal education. During the 22 years he had been with the firm, he had watched furiously as one fellow employee after another were promoted to posts which he felt he could fill as well *or better* than they. They had been promoted over him solely because they possessed a college degree which he himself lacked by three years. Time and again Bill had made up his mind to return to college at night, after work, and get that degree, but he dreaded tackling textbooks again. The long hours of sitting still, both in class and at home with his nose buried in tediously technical textbooks, and later to be subjected to nerve-wracking examinations on their endless factual contents, particularly now that he was 42, frightened him.

Working at the firm all day long was devitalizing enough, for his lower back grew so abominably tired long before the day was over that he could hardly concentrate. From the beginning of the day, too, Bill felt that nothing was ever right, no matter what he did. He felt that he needed a different office chair. Whenever he was standing, he felt like sitting, and whenever he was sitting, he felt like standing. When he was doing one thing, he left like doing another. And when he was doing that other thing, he felt like doing the first. Repeatedly, he felt as if a strange, indefinable weight was pressing against his lower back. It was followed by a vague numbness that made him restless and impelled him to get up and move around. When he got up, though, he felt stiff and weak-legged and wanted to sit down again. He tried stimulants, but their effects did not last long enough to be of practical value.

As a last resort, Bill went to his personal physician; then to an orthopedist, an osteopath, a chiropractor, and a naprapath. None found anything abnormally wrong with him. All advised him to exercise regularly, though, and to limit his intake of fatty foods and the like.

I firmly agreed with them. And then I thought along the lines of *sub*clinical disease: of disease *not yet* demonstrable by diagnosis and covered in no textbook . . . but a disease form nevertheless, *preceding* diagnosable disease. A disease *not yet* apparent to the conscious mind of the patient, but apparent to his *sub*conscious mind.

I taught Bill the Yogatone Replacer to firm up his lumbosacral joint, and the Yogatone Dorsal Arch to tone up his lower back muscles. He returned in two weeks and felt so much better in mind and body that he had signed up for night college. To his utter amazement, he did excellently, went straight through and graduated in two and a half years. Six months later, he was promoted to the post he wanted. Middle-aged, textbook frightened Bill had overcome his "uncontrollable" restlessness and returned to night college after work and made up, with little trouble, the credits he needed to advance in his career.

How High-Strung Randy Made Himself So Oblivious to His Surroundings that Nothing in Them Disturbed Him Any More

Randy, 48 years old, was obviously a high-strung man. He had been a bachelor until 41 and had married Wilma after his mother passed away. Once he had two children and dwelled near other families with children, his whole environment changed. Gone was the prized, dead-quiet surroundings of the bachelor life; the excessive maternal order about his apartment; the speak-in-your-turn conversation with his mother; the never-raised voices; the quiet arguing when opinions differed; the perfect regularity of his habits; the uninterrupted, perfectly-timed sleep. Now, the baby screamed at midnight; Wilma scolded Yvonne, the older child; Yvonne and her playmates were noisy in the backyard.

Randy's daily rest and his regular time for reading, doing his calisthenics or figuring his investments, was continuously interrupted to correct or admonish Yvonne, and yet not hurt her feelings. At the table, his own carefully planned eating was perpetually disturbed to supervise the children. There were scores of other disorganizing occurrences that he could not control. Yet, he *was* a loving family man. But he was being driven out of his mind trying to remake Wilma and the children just like him, for he had found that he could *not* remake himself to conform with them.

Randy's somewhat slumped (kyphotic) posture convinced me that he was exerting undue compression on his lower back. Nothing unusual, however, was revealed at diagnosis. Randy's somewhat slumped posture, though, compressed enough the naturally, abnormally narrow vertebral opening of his lumbo-sacral joint for it to squeeze significantly hard the spinal nerve passing through it and reduce the flow of its Spino-Volt. The longer he sat and read and went through his peaceful chores, the more his slumped posture reduced the Spino-Volt passing through that spinal nerve. Randy already complained of a restlessness to get up and move around whenever he sat for a short while. The reason was that his legs turned subliminally numb, and that his spinal nerve then flashed an emergency call to his subconscious mind to overcome the numbness. His subconscious mind replied by reflexly commanding the muscles of his legs to contract and *remove* the numbness, and so Randy was gripped with an unexplainable restlessness to get up and move around. Since that spinal nerve had been supersensitized by now by the constant harder squeezing it was enduring from his increasingly slumping posture, Randy's subconscious mind had been supersensitized by its messages also. His bachelor-trained mind was therefore easily upset by the usual annoyances of family life.

With the Yogatone Replacer he toned up the muscles of his lower back to support his lumbosacral joint, and it stopped flashing those urgent messages of irritation to his subconscious mind which maintained an unsuspected high-strung state. Thereafter, Randy was less reactive to the unavoidable annoyances of his comparatively new environment and became more philosophical about it.

Summary of the steps for using Yoga secrets for concentration

In order to apply Yoga secrets for concentration, you have to counteract the battering of the four horsemen on your lumbo-sacral joint in particular. Thus, you prevent your fastest wearing down joint from abnormally irritating your subconscious mind with vague discomforts from your lower back and filling your conscious mind with an unexplainable impatience, easily lost temper and ready quarrelsomeness. You achieve that by:

1. Reducing to the vanishing point the continuous irritation to your subconscious mind, with the Yogatone Replacer.
2. Toning up your lower back muscles and hip muscles with the Yogatone Dorsal Arch.
3. Making yourself mentally calm with the Yogatone Tranquilizer.

After you apply these Yoga secrets for a short time, the vague, lumbagoish, low-back pains vanish, and you regain a power to concentrate at any time and on any subject, which you never dreamed you possessed.

The Yoga Secrets for Self-Protection

7

Due to the lonely life he leads in distant places, the Yogi is constantly in need of self-protection. And since he carries no weapons, he is forced to rely upon himself alone. For thousands of years, as a result, he has evolved a special type of self-defense which requires little or no physical movement. For that reason, his self-protection secrets, like those of the iguana, are not secrets of body movement, so much as secrets of devitalizing the mind of his assailant by throwing it into confusion and consequent terror, through assuming certain secret stances which suggest far more than they are capable of doing. To insure that these secrets work at their best, however (like the iguana, again, and the fierce aspect it has evolved), the Yogi makes, first, two easy, but important, alterations of his body. His well-guarded self-protection secrets work then like magic, for they practically "freeze" his assailant to the ground. The case histories at the end of the chapter, prove how effective the Yogi's self-protection secrets can be for keeping you safe from the attacks of the biggest and most dangerous bullies.

How a big rib-box with its manly chest space
fills you with courage

Your spinal rib-joints (the joints formed between the back endings of your ribs and your spinal vertebrae) are the only joints in your body which *never rest* entirely (unless "fused together" by disease), so long as you are breathing and living. And since important nerves abut them, your spinal rib-joints can produce partial or complete paralysis of your abdominal muscles, as well as create some disturbances in the blood circulation of your abdomen, when they press upon these nerves, as they usually do when your rib-box droops under the ceaseless battering of the four horsemen. Many obscure symptoms then arise in your chest and abdomen, none of which may be diagnosable. When you take part in any effort, though, you find yourself easily winded and disheartened. No wonder that a drooped, cramped-in rib-box reduces your natural, inborn protective courage still further.

The Yogis found that nothing can fill you with more unconquerable courage than a big (for you), flexible rib-box. Such a rib-box widens your chest cavity and allows your heart and lungs more room to function. It massages the big veins of the lower half of your body, too, through the milking action of your diaphragm on them as it moves up and down around them when you breathe. The return of blood from your legs to your lungs and heart is greatly aided by that, thus reducing the load on your heart, and the dangers of your acquiring varicose veins. With the greater space available in your rib-box, too, for your lungs to expand, you regularly take in more oxygen and purify your blood faster. Working more efficiently, for all those reasons, your heart pumps blood, and withdraws waste-carrying blood, more efficiently from your brain. That lessens the possibilities of blood clots and other perils of blood stagnation. By moving down deeper when you breathe, also, your diaphragm massages your liver, your stomach, your spleen, your kidneys, your large and small intestines, and forces the waste matter to be more vigorously eliminated. The manly chest space, the expanded oxygen-intake and the flexible spinal rib-joints allow practically full Spino-Volt power to flow into your spinal nerves and into your muscles and fill you with natural, inborn, unconquerable courage.

The secret of acquiring a big rib-box for dynamic powering

If your chest is normal, your ribs, when at rest, slant down-wards from your spine, where they form the spinal rib-joints, at an angle of 15 to 20 degrees from the horizontal (*Figure 26—A*).

Figures 26A and B

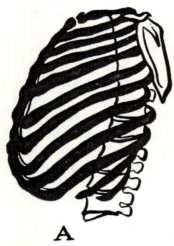 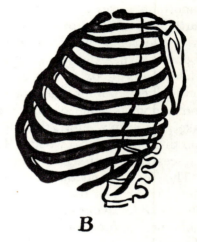

A

B

*Chest normal
ribs slant*

*Chest expanded
ribs more
nearly
horizontal*

When you expand your chest, your ribs are lifted closer to a right angle with your spine (*Figure 26—B*). Your whole breastbone, together with the whole front of your chest, is then lifted up-wards. In order to expand your chest, therefore, you have to lift your ribs higher than they are, and that necessitates muscle action.

When you breathe quietly, the muscles that lift your ribs con-sist of most of the muscles between them (the "spare-ribs meat" of the animal), and to a slight extent, of your diaphragm (which happens to be also a muscle). But the Yogis went far beyond this finding of the physiologists. They discovered their secret of *dynamic diaphragm piston-powering*. The Yogis found that, even after the lungs were fully expanded with air and the chest cavity raised, the chest could be elevated still further and enlarged *considerably more* by repeatedly applying to it dynamic, diaphragm piston-power a few minutes a day. With dynamic, diaphragm piston-power, I myself enlarged my own rib-box alone four inches in less than three months, without even exercising my back muscles or gaining weight! Within a few years I gained a total of 17 inches in chest size with additional rib-box expansion, plus developing my back and chest muscles with Yogametrics. (The muscles alone, it may be assumed, were responsible for about six inches of the total increase, and dynamic, diaphragm piston-powering for 11 inches.)

The basic secret of acquiring a big rib-box, with dynamic, diaphragm piston-powering is as follows:

1. Inhale deeply, first, and expand your rib-box fully.
2. Then, with your diaphragm, you push, or ram, this trapped air in your rib-box, from below, up against your chest wall, like a steam-engine piston hammering the steam trapped in the cylinder.
3. That stretches out your rib-box forcibly in all directions, even against the clutch of the torso muscles encircling it, which try to hold down its size. Repeat the procedure a few minutes a day, for weeks or months, and your ribs get longer (if you are still young enough), or remain up higher and higher and reward you with a noticeably bigger chest *without your even developing your chest or back muscles.* With a noticeably bigger chest you acquire a feeling of massiveness which you never possessed before, *even if you have not gained a pound of weight or muscle strength.* You also look *far more hefty and powerful* than you actually are. A bully's attitude towards you quickly turns more cautious. Your own courage zooms, as a result, and alters the whole situation in your favor.

How to prepare your rib-box for utmost expansion

To acquire a big rib-box and regain your lost natural, inborn, self-protection power fastest and easiest, apply scientifically perfected, dynamic, diaphragm piston-powering almost exactly as the Yogi does. That is, visualize it *while* you do it, and do it *just as* you visualize it. Follow that instruction to the letter!

All the time you are doing it, too, constantly bear in mind that, with it, you will press your air-filled lungs against *every single part* of your rib-box. You will press it against your diaphragm at the floor of it, against the sides of your chest, against the front of your chest, against the back of your chest, and against the top, flatter part of your chest closer to your neck. The top, flatter part of your chest is practically impossible to expand with deep breathing or exercise alone, and yet it is the part of your chest which is *most noticeable* to the eyes of others, particularly to the eyes of women and of bullies.

It is done most effectively on the Yogi Bench, as the Yogi does it.

The incomparable Yogi bench

The Yogi Bench is a well-guarded Yoga secret which certain masters have used for over 4,000 years to achieve many physical and physiological ends which Western man, with all his exact sciences and profuse experimentation, has not yet equalled. It is easy to make a Yogi Bench out of wood. (The Yogi himself used a smooth rock.) Just set a low stool or box, about half the height of the average chair, against a wall. (The Yogi set it against a tree trunk.) That is the Yogi Bench. There is no more to constructing it than that. But how effective it can be for bringing you untold benefits! Start using one without delay.

How to prepare your rib-box for utmost expansion fastest with the Yogi Bench

To prepare your rib-box for utmost expansion fastest with the Yogi Bench, follow these Yoga instructions closely (*Figure 27*).

1. Sit on the Yogi Bench, with your back normally straight.
2. Inhale slowly, deeply through your nose. (You automatically inhale slowly when you keep your mouth closed and inhale through your nostrils alone.) The air will fill the *base* of your lungs and spread out to the front and sides of your lower ribs.
3. Continue inhaling in the same manner, but now draw the air into the middle of your back, and fill up the *back* of your rib-box.
4. The front of the "chesty" part of your chest, though, also

Figure 27

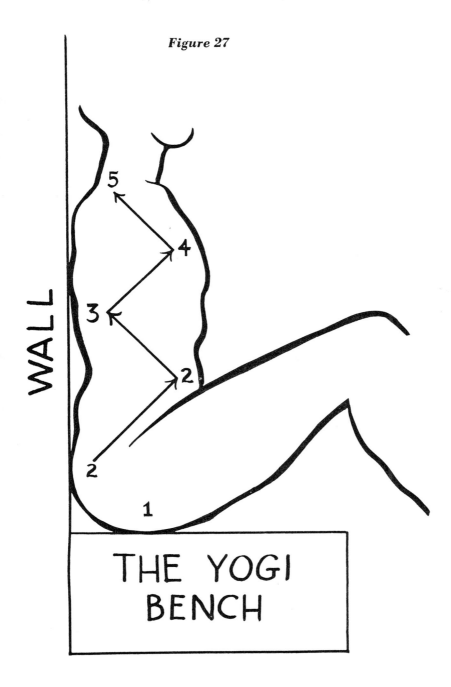

WALL

5
4
3
2
2
1

THE YOGI
BENCH

bulges somewhat now. So, continue inhaling and fill up both the front and the sides of your chest.

5. Draw the air into the *very roots* of your neck (or into the cone-like upper ends of your lungs), and fill the top, flatter part of your rib box.

6. Inhale still more air and fill your chest from top to bottom, so that it feels ready to burst.

Your diaphragm, which forms the floor of your chest cavity or rib-box, has ballooned out downwards to make room for the "bursting" air. You are ready to apply scientifically perfected, diaphragm piston-powering and acquire a big rib-box to regain your lost natural, inborn self-protection power.

How to apply dynamic, diaphragm piston-powering

To apply scientifically perfected, dynamic, diaphragm piston-powering:

1. Hold your breath now and contract your abdominal muscles. This forces your pushed-down diaphragm *upwards* into your rib-box, like a dynamic piston. In fact, *suck in* your diaphragm (just suck in your waist), so that you appear hollow at the waist and pop out at your chest (especially, at the *top half* of it). Since no air can escape through your windpipe now because you are holding your breath, your sucked-in diaphragm presses the trapped air in your rib-box, hard against its walls, thrusting them outwards in all directions. That enlarges your chest cavity still more, even though you are taking in no more air.

2. Enlarge your chest cavity *still more*, now, by sucking in your *lower ribs*. That squeezes air up from the mass of your lungs, into the top part of your burstingly expanded chest.

3. Keep your burstingly expanded chest in that state for three seconds. Then let out all the air.

Repeat this dynamic, diaphragm piston-powering 10 times daily, preferably in the morning upon arising. Your rib-box will expand more and more, each of the 10 times you repeat it, as its muscles and ligaments stretch to adjust to its larger girth to allow your lungs to take in more air.

NOTE: If you wish to build a gigantic rib-box for body building purposes and with startling speed, do scientifically perfected, dynamic, diaphragm piston-powering 15 minutes at a time in the morning upon arising, and in the evening before going to bed.

How diaphragm piston-powering relieves your tensions and lowers your blood pressure

Aside from giving you a big rib-box for self-protection purposes, dynamic, diaphragm piston-powering relieves your tensions and lowers your blood pressure. When you are under tension, your breathing is fast and shallow, and your breathing muscles, as a consequence, do not relax enough when you exhale. A certain amount of tension (residual tension) therefore remains in them. This residual tension is transmitted reflexly *directly into* the command-delivering nerves of other muscles neighboring your breathing muscles, *and it tenses those also.* The vicious circle repeats itself, reflexly, with one group of neighboring muscles after another, until your whole body is thrown into tension.

But that isn't all. Fast, shallow breathing *decreases* the normal activity of your diaphragm in milking the blood upwards from the veins of your legs, back to your lungs and heart. Blood, as a consequence, stagnates in your legs. That *increases* the load on your heart, fatiguing it unduly and thereby adding still more fatigue to your tensed body muscles. Dynamic, diaphragm piston-powering puts an end to your fast, shallow breathing and relaxes your breathing muscles fully. That allows them to exhale completely. The vicious circle is reversed at once, and the other tensed muscles of your body relax, too, reflexly. That eases the load from your heart and restores the normal circulation of your blood. It explains how systematic deep breathing causes a fall of blood pressure, and why it has been widely used to treat it. Dynamic, diaphragm piston-powering is deep breathing at its best.

The Yoga Chill: Yoga self-defense trick for "freezing" an attacker

Kantabahla, the slender, esthetic Yogi, was walking through the rough country of Assam, engrossed in deep meditation. He was suddenly accosted by a massive ruffian who was evidently migrating south to labor. Like most bullies, the ruffian had no obvious reason for bothering Kantabahla. Still, he swore and rushed at him, wielding the big stick he carried.

Although dwarfed by his assailant, Kantabahla just stood still. He just inhaled deeply and waited until the thug was within lunging distance. Kantabahla then suddenly dropped back about 15 inches on one foot (*Figure 28—A, B*) and faced him in the stance of a man ready to spring at him and rip him apart. The bully paused. Kantabahla remained where he was, but crouched a little more and opened his hands wider, as if preparing to leap savagely. With dynamic, diaphragm piston-powering, he subtly enlarged his chest by several inches for a moment or two. The attacker surveyed him, apparently nonplussed, then stepped back a little. Kantabahla edged forwards at once, as if to remain within leaping distance. The disconcerted brawler stepped further back, but Kantabahla still kept close enough to him, purposely looking impatient to demolish him. Time, Kantabahla realized, was on his side, for the longer he puzzled his foe, the sooner would his foe lose his confidence and pugnacity. To speed up matters, Kantabahla pretended to assume the aggressive stance now himself by gripping the air with his fingers and peering at his enemy as if he contemplated doing something murderous. The bully's big stick trembled in his hands, his face turned pale, and his eyes bulged. Immediately, he called for a truce. With the Yoga Chill, the slender, esthetic Kantabahla had frozen his attacker to the ground helplessly. Practice it yourself, to be ready to use it on any ruffian who may attack you.

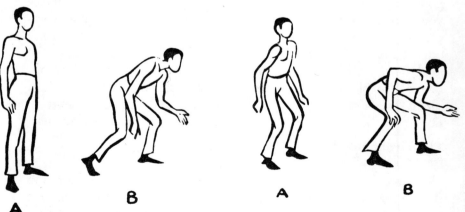

A   B   A   B

Figure 28   *Figure 29*

The Yoga Rout: the Yoga self-defense trick for confounding an assailant and changing his mind about attacking you

Laplangah, a Yogi, was once passing a village in western India. The poverty-stricken inhabitants suspected every stranger, for every stranger was usually hungry and was ready to steal food. A towering villager, accordingly, ordered Laplangah not to set foot within the place. When Laplangah ignored him, the big villager started for him.

Laplangah at once stepped back about 15 inches with his right leg and leaned back on it (*Figure 29—A*). Then he crouched low swiftly and rubbed his front knee, as if preparing to do something devastating with it (*Figure 29—B*). (The Yogi's main object in self-protection is to *always halt the first rush or move* of his assailant, and to accomplish that by doing something that not only puzzles his assailant, but also alarms him. The expectation of an easy, unopposed conquest is then replaced in the bully's mind by the prospect of a long, uncertain, and perhaps disastrous struggle. And since every bully is basically a coward, he is promptly gripped with terror.)

To keep him uncertain and bewildered, Laplangah made a sudden move with his front leg, as if preparing to leap with a crushing kick.

The same procedure was repeated several times. At long last, the villager asked Laplangah softly whether he desired to enter the village. With the Yoga Rout, the Yoga self-defense trick, Laplangah had confounded an assailant by changing his mind about attacking him, without bodily contact.

NOTE: As the Yogis contend, you don't have to participate actively, if at all, in a physical struggle, to overcome your enemy. You overcome him most easily by throwing his mind into such confusion *by what you make him think you might do to him* that he promptly changes his diabolical attitude towards you and thinks of his own safety first.

Practice the two simple, but unbelievably effective, Yoga self-defense tricks yourself in private, especially before a mirror, and so be always ready to vanquish a bully without bodily contact.

Case histories

> HOW "SKIN-AND-BONES" JEFFORDS, WHO HAD BEEN
> SEVERELY BEATEN UP BY A BULLY, MADE HIM
> KEEP OUT OF HIS WAY THEREAFTER

"Skin-and-Bones" Jeffords was a slightly-built young clerk who, like so many other bachelors in the big city, frequented social clubs. It was an easy way to meet companions in the big town. Finally Jeffords met a girl who attracted him immensely, but he was muscled out of the way by a rough type of man whom the girl apparently wanted nothing to do with. Jeffords asked him to leave her alone, but the rough became rowdy, and the bartender came over and warned him against bothering the girl.

When Jeffords started out that night, the bully hurried after him and beat him to a pulp.

Jeffords was afraid to return to the club to meet that girl again. He was not eager to study self-defense tricks, though. He wished only that he could rid himself of that bully with merely a look.

I taught Jeffords how to expand his rib-box with dynamic, diaphragm piston-powering, as well as how to equalize the heights of his shoulders. In three months he had gained three inches in rib-box girth alone, and the new "chesty" feeling it gave him left him feeling much bigger and stronger than he was.

Jeffords returned to the club, and the girl was there again! She threw him a glowing look the moment he entered, as if she was waiting eagerly for his return. Jeffords had hardly settled down beside her, though, when the bully entered the place, perceived him and marched over at once and ordered him away. Jeffords arose slowly, taking a deep breath as he did so. Then he subtly expanded his chest several inches with dynamic, diaphragm piston-powering. Aside from the much more impressive figure it suddenly carved of him, it gave him a "chesty feeling" and put a calm, confident look in his eye.

The ruffian's jaw dropped. Jeffords, meanwhile, exhaled quietly, but still kept his chest expanded. His enemy turned pale and sputtered, then slowly withdrew.

As Jeffords escorted the girl out of the club that night, to take her home, they passed the bully near the door. But he pretended not to see them. Again and again Jeffords took the girl to that club after that, but his enemy kept his distance. "Skin-and-Bones" Jeffords, who had been once severely beaten up by a bully, had made the ruffian keep out of his way thereafter.

Summary of the steps for using Yoga for self-protection

In order to apply the Yoga secrets for self-protection, you have to counteract the battering of the four horsemen of the mastabah on the full length of your spine and rib-box. Thus, you counteract the forming of wrong-back curves which leave the heights of your shoulders uneven (no matter if the unevenness is not readily detected by the eye), and your rib-box dropping and significantly shrinking the natural size of your chest. Your vertebral openings will then be narrowed as little as possible, allowing the spinal nerves passing through them to push powerful enough Spino-Volts through to your muscles to meet any emergency and fill you with unconquerable courage. You also look much more hefty and powerful than you actually are and, consequently, disconcert the bully without making a move. You achieve all this by:

1. Acquiring a big rib-box with manly chest space and considerably expanded oxygen-intake, by using dynamic, diaphragm piston-powering.
2. Equalizing the tone of your unevenly developed shoulder and back muscles with Yogatone and thereby evening your shoulder heights as much as possible.
3. Using the Yoga Chill, the Yoga self-defense trick for "freezing" an attacker.
4. Using the Yoga Rout, the Yoga self-defense trick for confounding an attacker and changing his mind about you without bodily contact.

You will soon possess the "chest" and the confidence to stop the bully so fast that he halts his first rush at you before it even gets fully started. You are therefore protected against him without even striking a blow through special secrets of Yoga.

Yoga Secrets for Greater Personal Energy

8

One of the foremost necessities of a Yogi is energy—living as he does, without luxuries, conveniences or help, in a merciless environment, and without clothes or proper food or physician's care if he loses his health. Therefore, the Yogi is compelled to develop energy little short of a superhuman, to meet any obstacle he encounters, even in his regular daily life. His rigorous disciplines also demand ceaseless energy, for he spares himself no effort or discomfort in his programs to attain his goals. The Yogi, as a result, is a master in the ways of developing superhuman energy for instant use at any age. His secrets for energy have been carefully studied and refined for *your own use* in the practical Western world, to enable you to fill yourself with energy for your everyday life with comparative speed and ease, without subjecting yourself to wearisome disciplines. The case histories following the exercises prove how effective they can be for bringing you unsurpassable energy with safety and unbelievable speed.

How the four horsemen diminish your natural, inborn energy

1. Causing strain on your body (particularly back strain) which mercilessly depletes your natural, inborn energy.
2. Converting your spine into a weakened and distorted "accordion torso."

3. Bringing on muscle-spasm imbalance which robs you of your daily vitality.
4. Causing diaphragmatic ptosis (dropped diaphragm).
5. Victimizing you with the telltale, end of the day "gel."

You will now be shown how the four horsemen bring on these unwanted changes in you and diminish your natural, inborn energy, as well as the scientifically perfected Yoga secrets for counteracting them.

How strain (particularly back strain) mercilessly wastes and lowers your natural, inborn energy

Strain—particularly the unyielding, persistent strain of gravity, of faulty posture, and the intermittent strain of weight-bearing and ground resistance—wastes and lowers your natural, inborn energy by overworking and fatiguing the ligaments and muscles of your whole body, especially those of your hips and torso. A strain is a minor injury which is normally rapidly repaired when the tissues involved are rested and allowed to heal. Chronic strains, though, are those which are *not* allowed to heal, and they are regularly inflicted on the body. Strains inflict minor tears so small in the affected tissues that they produce a pain which is more irritating to the *subconscious mind*, than it is sharp and crippling to the parts affected. But your subconscious mind grows increasingly sensitive to that pain in the course of time, and wastes much of your energy suppressing the unpleasant sensation.

You can strain your back when you engage in heavy weight-bearing, or when you engage in light weight-bearing while holding a position of poor body balance. That's why back strain frequently occurs when people try to open windows.

Every occupation produces strain, because every occupation involves the use, overuse or abuse of certain tissues. Each occupation therefore creates its own peculiar and particular type of physical trouble. Railroad workers and foremen are subject to fractures and dislocations. Those employed in shoveling, or running hoisting machinery, strain certain hip ligaments and develop low-back pain. In industrial workers, two-thirds of the injuries occur in the lumbosacral region, and 11 percent of them are sacroiliac sprains. Golf is a common cause of low-back strain, and practicing it causes more strain than playing it, particularly with short-distance clubs.

Not only the ligaments, but also the muscles, of the vertebrae are subject to strain, fatigue, rupture or inflammation. The chief traumatic causes of backache are, in the following order: *strain*, followed by sprain, concussion, contusion, rupture of soft tissues like muscles, compression, crushing, displacements, hemorrhage and avulsions. The chief industrial causes of disabilities of the back are sprains, strains, fractures and dislocations.

THE MAN MOST VULNERABLE

The type of man who is vulnerable to the extremely painful "locked back" syndrome (or to the utmost torture in strain) is usually the overworked man between 45 and 55 who, for years, has been under mental and physical strain. His only sport is weekend golf, sedentary car driving, private plane flying or motorboating. He is usually overweight, eats too much meat and polysaturated fatty foods, drinks beer and coffee instead of water, and is on the verge of gout. He has endured many attacks of lumbago, bursitis of the shoulder, acid stomach and sore arches. He smokes, is a "heel walker" and "works on his home" for exercise. The ligaments and muscles of his back, shoulders, hips, knees and ankles are weak from disuse and are subject easily to the most severe strain, or to the excruciatingly painful syndrome of feeling as if his back is "locked."

Any kind of strain robs your body of its natural, inborn energy. Even the subliminal strain resulting constantly from the four horsemen of the mastabah plagues your body with a wearisome, irritating, frustrating sensation which flashes to your subconscious mind messages of helplessness and surrender. Your subconscious mind reacts to them by wasting your natural nerve-electricity power (your natural Spino-Volt) by steadily delivering unperceived commands to the muscles of your body to go into mild spasm to support the strained part or parts. That's how strain—particularly, back strain, because the spine is the energy pipeline —wastes and lowers your natural, inborn energy.

"The accordion torso" effect on your spine

The four horsemen, as you already know, start trampling you

down the moment you assume the two-footed position and distort the shape, and devitalize the natural, inborn energy of, your torso as it vainly combats them. In the course of time your spine is crushed and twisted downwards by them like an accordion, known as "the accordion back." The structures that "settle" in your back are its disks, vertebral joints, muscles, ligaments and vertebrae. You experience, as a result, a dull pain in your back, which is aggravated by standing, and relieved only partially by rest. The dull pain may not even be perceived by your conscious mind, but you go through life with mysterious, alternating periods of comfort and discomfort. The condition, for that reason, is a frequent cause of *psychoneurosis*, which is insidious in its onset, and "often subconscious and innocent."

The "accordionating" of your back, in fact, takes place from the time you get up in the morning, until you go to bed at night, during which time your overnight re-elongated spine "buckles" during the day and shrinks your height (in some cases several inches).

How diaphragmatic ptosis (dropped diaphragm) seriously diminishes your natural, inborn energy

Once your back is "settled," "buckled" or "accordionated," your rib-box collapses forwards and downwards with it, compressing and twisting its contents (your heart, your lungs, and their covering sheaths) into tortured masses of outraged flesh. The muscles of your weak, tone-less diaphragm below it are unable to cope with this avalanche of carnage piling down upon it, and stretch downwards abnormally under the load and flatten out somewhat and strain the visceral organs beneath it. That is diaphragmatic ptosis (*Figures 30, 31*). These victimized visceral organs include your stomach, small intestines, spleen, colon, kidneys, adrenal glands, pancreas, bladder, big and small blood vessels, your solar plexus and all the nerves composing it, and still more. Your whole torso, in other words, both from within and without, is now mis-shapen and smashed into a near chaotic, anatomical mass.

Following are some of the resulting structural catastrophes which distort your torso then, due to the "accordionation" of your back.

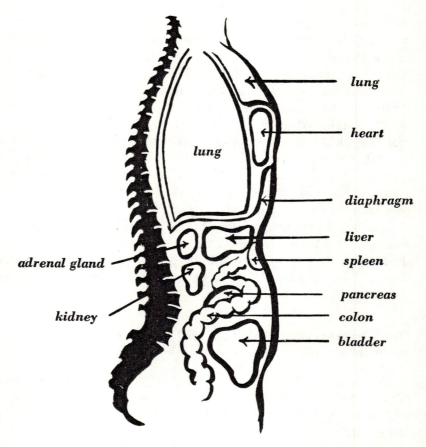

Figure 30: Normal Diaphragm

A. DUE TO THE DROPPING FORWARDS AND
DOWNWARDS OF YOUR RIB-BOX,

1. There is a resulting undue pulling on your esophagus (gullet), producing symptoms like lumps in your throat (globus hystericus).

2. There is excessive stretching of the nerves of your gullet, as well as upon the parasympathetic nerves as they descend from your head to command the natural functions of your visceral organs. That reduces the natural functioning of all these organs.

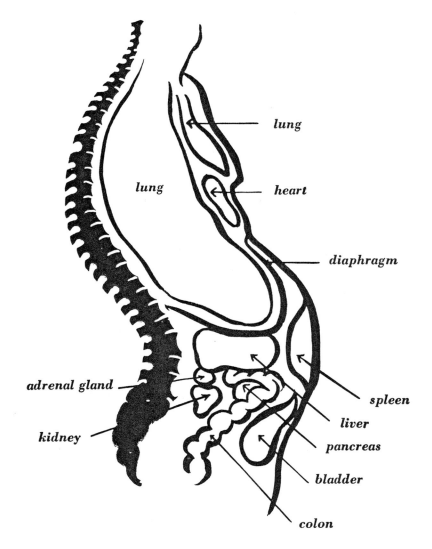

Figure 31: Fallen Diaphragm
(Diaphragmatic Ptosis)

3. There is a resulting unusual pulling downwards on the
   coverings of your lungs (your pleura) and of your heart
   (your pericardium). Your heart itself is twisted, but that
   will be explained later.

B. DUE TO THE PUSHING DOWN OF YOUR WEAK, TONE-LESS
   DIAPHRAGM BY YOUR DROPPING RIB-BOX AND ITS
   CONTENTS, INTO YOUR ABDOMINAL CAVITY,

4. There is excessive stretching of the sympathetic nerves which control the blood supply of your abdominal organs.

5. The return of the blood from your legs to your lungs and heart is slowed down by 20 to 30 per cent, because your overstretched diaphragm cannot contract and rise as much as it should when you breathe, to milk your inferior vena cava, the vein through which the blood returns from your lower body to your heart.

6. Your upper abdominal visceral organs (your stomach, spleen, liver, smaller intestines) are unduly compressed.

7. The size of your abdominal cavity is reduced (since its floor cannot move down further to make room for the excessive compression from above). The resulting congestion of your visceral organs leaves you prone to hernia, blood stagnation in your liver, and varicose veins.

8. Your liver, in fact, in order to fit into the reduced abdominal space, tends to be rotated counter-clockwise, as well as to be wedged down upon your right kidney below it.

9. The lower curve of your stomach sags markedly on the left, leaving you prone to belching, burping, having an acid taste in your stomach and regurgitating a lot.

10. Your stomach sag will press down abnormally on your pancreas; while your pancreas will, in turn, be wedged downwards and backwards upon the blood vessels of your spleen.

11. Deep within your abdominal cavity, there is dropping, clumping and pooling of your small intestines. That hinders the normal "pushing onwards" of your food during digestion.

12. There is extraordinary pulling and stretching of the nerves and blood vessels that go to, and leave from, your intestinal loops.

13. There is abnormal pressure upon your urinary bladder and rectum from above, causing them to turn backwards, or to clump low, in the floor of your abdomen (known as your pelvic basin).

14. The visceral organs of your lower abdomen and pelvis

drop, pressing down upon the arteries and veins of your hip region (your iliacs). That causes or aggravates the slowed blood circulation of your legs, which inclines you still more to varicose veins and hemorrhoids.

15. The attachments and the positions of many of your visceral organs are changed or altered, disturbing their natural functions, as well as those of their nerve and blood supply.

And that's just the beginning of what these resulting anatomical catastrophies can lead to! You can readily understand, then, how diaphragmatic ptosis seriously diminishes your natural, inborn energy—*even when there is no diagnostic pain or any other clinical symptom of disease.* Why? Because, to stretch normal tissues abnormally, and persistently, and for no beneficial purpose, brings on body tissue calamities! To quote a warning given to surgeons for back surgery: "Stretching of tissues does more harm than cutting them."

The final blow: the telltale end of the day gel

Your convincing daily reminder that you are buckling under your "settled" back and diaphragmatic ptosis, is your telltale day end gel. This is the pain and stiffness which you experience regularly in your back after resuming activity following a period of rest or sedentary activity such as after you play cards; get out of a bus, car, plane, train or other conveyance after a long ride; or after you sit all day at your desk or worktable, truck or bulldozer. Your movements are then stiff and awkward, often accompanied by pain.

This condition affects everybody to a degree under similar circumstances; but, it is accentuated, and takes more time to dissipate, when you possess a "settled" back and consequent muscle spasms and diaphragmatic ptosis. The telltale end of the day gel results mainly because the muscles, ligaments and fasciae (fibrous-sheaths enveloping the muscles) of your back have shortened when you sat or rested. When they are suddenly stretched again as you arise and move before they are warmed up, and before enough of their normal blood circulation has been restored, they resist being stretched out limberly so fast and *contract* somewhat instead.

That produces the stiffness you feel. It also limits the freedom of your movements, forcing you to move about awkwardly, weakly, and unsure of yourself. The direct cause is that the tissues of your muscles, ligaments and fasciae have sort of "gelled"—or changed from their normal liquid, or semi-liquid, protoplasmic state—into a more rubbery, or jelly-like state, due to their recent inactivity and to their consequently receiving less liquid supply from their considerably reduced normal blood circulation. Your natural, inborn energy is sapped still more by it.

How to regain your inborn energy with Yogatone

With Yogatone you overcome your diaphragmatic ptosis, enlarge your rib-box and help smooth out your wrong-back curves. Yogatone helps push back your fallen organs to their natural positions, free your blood vessels from undue compression, release your jammed vertebrae from their fixed positions in your wrong-back curves, and allow those vertebral joints again to bear weight competently. Yogatone relieves the abnormal tensions upon the ligaments of those joints and equalizes the tone of the muscles on both sides of them, thereby helping to eliminate the spasms of their muscles. Yogatone re-elongates your spine by de-accordionating it as much as possible, thus widening its narrowed vertebral openings and freeing the spinal nerves that pass through them, from the abnormal squeeze against them. The Yogatone Visceral Replacer, the ergo-lat 45 and the Double Drive achieve all that for you and regain for you lost, natural, inborn energy (*Figures 32, 33, 34, 35, 36*).

How to tone up your energy-releasing chest muscles with Yogatone

THE DOUBLE DRIVE (*Figures 34, 35, 36*).

The DOUBLE DRIVE is an unusual, easy, and most effective chest and abdominal muscle toner and developer. It is done exactly as the Yogis do it, too.

You stand and double hook the "person" you imagine standing in front of you, with both hands at the same time. Keep your elbows *close to your body* all the way.

Round your whole torso, from neck to knees, forwards. Round your shoulders, too. This rounding contracts your chest and

Figure 32: The Yogatone Visceral Replacer

squeezes visceral organs into
place and forces them upwards

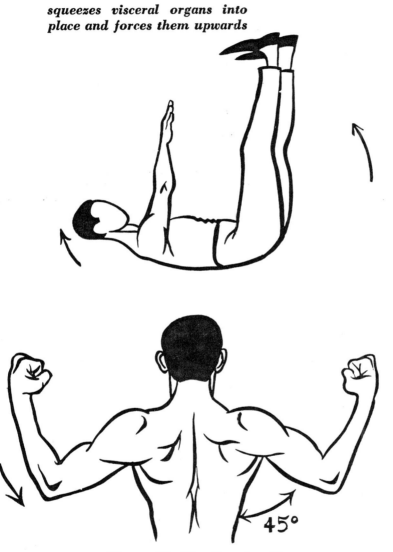

Figure 33: The Ergo-lat 45

stand or sit with back straight. bend elbows
and spread arms out 45° from body. contract hard, downwards

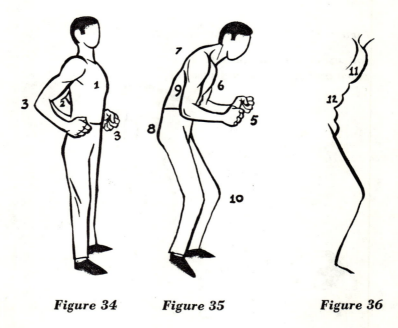

Figure 34   *Figure 35*   *Figure 36*

abdominal muscles at their best angles of pull. Forcibly contract them at the same time that you round your shoulders, and exhale.

This simple movement, also, builds up your chest and flattens your belly in surprisingly short time. It also develops your arms and forearms, is a fine massager of your spine and lungs, and is an excellent aid to simple, uncomplicated constipation.

Frequency

Do it from 2 to 5 times a day, exactly as described in Figures 34, 35, 36.

The position to assume (Figure 34).

1. Take a deep breath.
2. Straighten your back.
3. Draw arms back, with fists clenched.

How to do this exercise (Figure 35).

4. Now, bring your arms forwards, inwards and upwards in an arc.

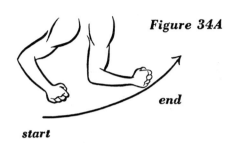

Figure 34A

end

start

5. Bring arms forward forcibly, as if striking two body blows at the same time (Also *Figure 34*).
6. At the same time exhale,
7. Round your back,
8. Round your hips,
9. Hollow your chest,
10. Bend your knees, and contract your
11. Chest muscles and
12. Your abdominal muscles (*Figure 36*).

Case histories

How Elmer, When Fatigued After a Full Day's Work, Recharged Himself with Energy by Toning Up His Energy-Releasing Back Muscles

Elmer was in his middle forties, and was exhausted at the end of his working day. His back felt as if crushed by an overwhelming weight, and ached numbly in places. His shoulders hung, pushing his rib-box down to his waist. From the seat of his hips to his neck, his back described a weary, tone-less, bending arc, and his chest and abdomen slid down almost into his lap. So fatigued did he feel that he didn't care if he ever moved again.

With long-awaited relief, nonetheless, Elmer staggered to his feet at "quitting" time. But he could hardly straighten his body. His knees felt locked, and his back was so agonizingly stiff that he expected never to straighten it again. His chest had caved-in and flattened so low that his clothes were roomy in the upper half of his torso. He had hardly energy left to put on his hat and coat.

Elmer had been driven to taking stimulants to pep himself up after work, but had grown alarmed because he was becoming addicted. He went to several different doctors for check-ups. All found him organically sound, but each one advised him to exercise regularly. But Elmer was too weary at the end of the day. Many tasks usually awaited him after work, besides. Sometimes he had to work overtime, attend night school, go out with his family, or even repair something for the home.

Realizing that Elmer would not continue long with a program of exercises, I taught him the Yoga back toners for quick energy (the ergo-lat and the ergo-back 45), and advised him to do them on the Yogi Bench, whenever he could. Otherwise, to do them just on his regular work, or office, chair They would take up only a few seconds of his time.

Elmer did them the very next day, right after work, when he had to stay again overtime. He was amazed at the wave of warm energy that flashed across his back almost immediately, and how swiftly the sensation that his back had been pounded mercilessly with the wide surface of a plank, vanished. He felt, in fact, as if suddenly reborn, and he tackled the overtime with the optimism that he would not be exhausted by it. The psychological impact alone filled him with ecstasy. From then on, he regularly stimulated his waning energy with those Yoga movements and changed into such a different person that he actually begged me for more such movements for his whole body.

How listless, discouraged, unemployed Rogers recharged himself with energy by increasing his Spino-Volt

Rogers had done rather well in life until 52. He had been employed regularly, had raised five children and paid off the mortgage on the family home. His two eldest children were nearly through college, and his younger three were in high school.

Then the world caved in on him. First, Edna, his wife, required a costly operation that could not be postponed long. Secondly, either as a result of a company merger or automation, Rogers found himself out of work. For the next year, he hounded the employment offices and replied to one want ad after another— but, all to no avail. He seemed *too old* to find a new job.

Before long, Rogers' savings were reduced to the point where they could provide only about a few months' living for the family.

From then on, Rogers drifted from one desperate mood to another. He felt listless, discouraged and energy-sapped, as if his manly honor were at stake. His chest sank lower and lower, his back bent deeper and deeper, and he took more and more stimulants to pep himself up. His occupation had "humped" his back a little, but it was increasingly noticeable now. Now, too, he experienced continually a dragging, pulling sensation from his whole torso, as if he were wearily carrying a sack of potatoes on his shoulders. His spirits sank so low, and he turned so lethargic to everything in general that, Edna, who knew me, persuaded him to have a talk with me.

Since his doctor had found him to be in fairly good health, I felt that renewing his energy would make a new man of him. So I had Rogers tone up the muscles of his chest and back a few times with Yogatone. Quickly, he enjoyed enough of an overall physical hardness to make him feel again like the rock of the home. Then I had him raise his diaphragm and reposition his sunken organs a little with The Yogatone Visceral Replacer (previously described) and allow his heart and lungs more room to function and lessen the wearying, distorting pull on them. He felt as if the strangling strait-jacket around his torso had been loosened a little, and his conscious mind swiftly filled with a renewed optimism about life which he had long lost. And so he soon accepted the past as *past*, and the present and future as new portions of his life which had to be faced independently.

Rogers, with renewed energy coursing through him, experimented and came up with an inexpensive, but useful, little gadget for a common, leisure time sport, and offered it by mail. The response surpassed his expectations. He immediately procured supplies, manufactured the gadget by hand in his basement and expanded his advertising once it was tested. He sold more and and more. He added two or three variations of the gadget to his list, and by the end of the year was doing so well that he considered hiring two part-time helpers.

Summary of the steps for using Yoga secrets for energy

In order to apply Yoga secrets for energy, you have to counteract the straining of the muscles and ligaments of your spine and diaphragm, and the resulting "buckling" and "accordionating" of your spine which throw your visceral organs out of proper position and crowd them against each other, culminated by the telltale end of the day gel. You do so with Yogatone by:

1. Using the Yogatone Visceral Replacer to help reduce backstrain, de-accordionate your torso, relieve muscle-spasm imbalance and lift your dropped diaphragm and your fallen visceral organs back to their natural positions.
2. Toning up your flabby chest muscles with the Double Drive.
3. Toning up your flabby back muscles with the ergo-lat and the ergo-dorsal 45.

Simple movements 2 and 3 will release the dormant energy contained in those unused muscles of yours and flash the sensation to your conscious mind. Your conscious mind will then automatically order your subconscious mind to stimulate your sympathetic nervous system (and your adrenal glands) and fill you with energy swiftly.

Yoga Secrets for Powerful Muscles

9

Although the Yogi spends considerable time sitting and meditating, he undertakes long, arduous journeys repeatedly, either to visit another master, or just to settle elsewhere. Since he travels by foot through rough, perilous terrain, and has to do so speedily or risk starvation, he needs extraordinary muscle power to climb and descend steep precipices, to swim across the currents of rushing rivers, to climb high trees for food, to leap across wide, death-threatening gorges, to outrun groups of ruffians stalking the trails. And he has to commence the journey with bulky enough muscles, to avoid turning helpless before it is over. The Yogi prepares himself for such an undertaking by enormously increasing his muscle bulk and power—even if it is not apparent in his garb. He does it in record time, too, with the secrets handed down from master to master over thousands of years. These have been carefully studied and refined for *your own use* to enable you to develop Mr. America-type muscles with comparative speed and ease, without subjecting yourself to strenuous efforts. The case histories prove how effective they can be for bringing you big, powerful muscles with safety, minimum effort, and unbelievable speed.

How your inborn muscle size and power is depleted

The four horsemen of the mastabah reduce your natural, inborn muscle size and power by:

1. Their steady wear-and-tear on your spinal disks.
2. The resulting narrowing of your vertebral openings, which reduces the Spino-Volt of the commands which your conscious and subconscious minds deliver to your muscles.
3. Your ignorance of the best angle of pull for developing each muscle to its peak fastest, and with the least effort.
4. Your not knowing the secret of Yogametrics, and how to use it to acquire muscle power and bulk swiftly.

You will now be shown how the above unwanted changes come upon you and reduce your natural, inborn muscle bulk and power. Then, the refined, scientifically-perfected Yoga secrets for counteracting them and developing big, powerful muscles will be set out for you.

**How the four horsemen steadily wear
down your cushiony, vertebral openings and disks**

Your spine is a flexible, upright, segmented column with 25 vertebral joints. Like your pubic-joints, your vertebral-joints are joints of slight movement, but they need great strength. Such joints for that reason are bound together by tough and elastic fibrocartilages. The fibrocartilages of your vertebral-joints are sandwiched between the cylindrical bodies of adjacent vertebrae and are called *spinal disks*. They form the chief bands that bind the bodies of neighboring vertebrae together. Thus, they form an integral part of your vertebral joints and permit movement between your individual vertebrae. They also transmit your body weight.

Different parts of your spinal disks afford stability to your spine; and they absorb shock, permit fluid exchange between your vertebrae and the disks themselves, and equalize stress. Your spinal disks afford your spine one-quarter of its length, provide some 40 percent of its movement, and help provide it with its normal curves. They also provide it with a sensation of body movement and position. A vertical line drawn through the shock-absorbing pulp in the center of each of your spinal disks will pass through the weight-bearing axis of your spine. Your spinal disks, in fact, are like noncompressible struts which hold and keep your vertebral bodies separated. The amount of positive pressure, too, which an intact spinal disk can stand, as well as the amount of vertebral compression necessary to rupture it, is surprising. When a 200 pound man is standing, his last spinal disk alone (the one in the lumbosacral joint at the base of his spine) supports nearly 120 pounds of his weight!

You *can* rupture or tear one of your spinal disks, though, when you subject it to enough trauma because, when you bend forward or backward, the pulp of your spinal disk is squeezed into one direction or the other, forcing your spinal disk to "bulge out" in the opposite direction. Indeed, when your spine is subjected to unusual stress or strain such as from bearing too heavy a weight, or from resisting too strong a pull, your spinal disk may rupture and extrude its pulp backwards into your spinal canal. (This is erroneously called a "slipped disk.") Daily, continuous unsuspected wear-and-tear from the four horsemen, however, continuously and insidiously grind down your spinal disks. Your vertebral openings, as a result, are narrowed all the more, tightening their squeeze on your spinal nerves. *That lessens the Spino-Volt Power of the messages your spinal nerves carry from your body to your brain*, and the commands they deliver from your brain to your body. The best way to save your spinal disks from this constant wear-and-tear on them would be by rotating them, just as the auto expert advises you to rotate your car wheels every three months to avoid uneven wear-and-tear on the wheels, especially the tires. Even if that could be done, though, the wear-and-tear on your spinal disks would still continue because every move you make creates centrifugal force (for example, twists, rotation and torsion-torque), and that continues the wear-and-tear on your spinal disks.

How weight-bearing affects your spine and diminishes your muscle strength and bulk

During your youth, while your spinal disks still have blood supply, your normal exercise movements feed your vertebrae beneficially. When you bend forward, backward, twist or bend sidewise, lift or bear weight, jump, run, breathe deeply and so on, your vertebral openings are continually widened and narrowed during the activity, for they are not fixed openings, but flexible. That's why they are called openings of changing diameters. Their contents, in other words, are then alternately compressed harder by the vertebral openings when these are narrowed (as occurs when you lift weight), or are stretched when the vertebral openings are widened (as occurs when you stretch your back, bend or twist your body). This alternate compressing and stretching of the contents of your vertebral openings (that is, of your spinal nerves and of the blood and lymph vessels that supply your vertebrae) in normal movement, gently massages and stimulates them. It also pumps more blood into your vertebrae, and pumps away faster their waste-carrying blood. The flat, cushiony spinal disks sandwiched in between your vertebrae, meanwhile, permit your vertebrae to move and rotate when you move, without letting your vertebral openings narrow so much that they squeeze their contents steadily and hinder their functions.

Once you are an adult, however, the picture changes. Your spinal disk has lost its blood vessels by then and, consequently, has no blood supply. It therefore cannot repair itself when damaged from injury or daily wear-and-tear. Neither does it possess nerves of pain. From your late 40's on, besides, your spinal disk starts hardening and losing its elasticity and its shock-absorbing capacity and becoming more prone to "disk slipping" (or extrusion of the pulp of the disk) upon weight-bearing. And that *is* a common threat because stress on the vertebrae of your lower back sometimes equals 2000 pounds. As the wear-and-tear on your spinal disks proceeds over the years, gradually limiting your movements more and more, you experience, occasionally, subliminal pain and slight stiffness in your back.

Heavy straining or lifting are not the only causes of the steady wear-and-tear, either. Equally to blame are the daily wrong uses of your back in repeated wrong bending, wrong turning and weight-bearing, with their microtraumatic (repeated small) injuries. When you turn, it's the twist or stretch on your spinal disks that wears them down.

Your spinal disks which wear-and-tear the most are the two close to the base of your neck, and the two at the base of your spine. Those are the regions in which you should take unusual pains to prevent your spinal disks from wearing down and causing you not only severely narrowed vertebral openings and maddening pain, but also serious back trouble. That's why the Yoga secrets had to be refined and made scientific for you before you could use them safely.

Your spinal disks, naturally, are also worn down by heavy weight-bearing—and to such a degree that they could eventually weaken you disastrously or even cripple you. There are famous weight-lifters who, already when comparatively young men, suffer severely from back and knee trouble. Others risk suffering from them later.

Use of Yogametrics

Refraining from physical activity, though, will not help, because your bones then turn more porous, decrease in size in time, and your muscles not only shrink considerably, but a significant percentage of their normal mass degenerates into permanent fat. Yogametrics is the scientific way to develop big, powerful muscles faster and easier, while at the same time sparing your spinal disks from excessive wear-and-tear. Yogametrics achieves that ideal because it depends hardly at all upon disk-traumatizing weight-bearing for muscle development, but almost completely upon using the muscle's best angle of pull.

The advantage of using the best angle of pull of the muscle to make it big and strong surprisingly fast

A joint is dominated by the muscles which act across it. The joint exists for the muscle, not the muscle for the joint. The position in which a muscle starts to work is its "zero point" or weakest point. The muscle is strongest midway between the full range of its contraction, where its "moment of force" is at its maximum.

The more parallel the ending of a muscle is to the axis of the bone in which it is inserted, the weaker is its action. The muscle is at its strongest when its insertion forms a *right angle* with the bone. That's why a high-peaked, developed muscle has *more power* than a low-peaked, undeveloped muscle. For example, when your elbow is either flexed or extended, the power of your brachialis muscle is at its weakest. Its power is at its strongest when your forearm forms a *right angle* with your upper arm, for then your brachialis muscle is almost at right angles to its insertion in your forearm. That is its *best angle of pull.*

YOGAMETRICS VS. ISOMETRICS

Yogametrics enables you easily to contract your muscles at their peaks in their best angles of pull. You cannot do that with weights because weights are so heavy and bulky that you have to balance or heave them when you handle them. Neither can you do that with isometric exercises because with isometrics you contract your muscles at the *end* of their movements, or when their contractions are *well past* their best angles of pull. Only with Yogametrics, as the Yogis discovered long ago, can you easily contract *any* muscle strongest at its right contraction angle, or at its *best angle* of pull, and therefore at its angle of *greatest strength.* Only with Yogametrics, then, can you contract the greatest number of muscle fibers of your muscles at their peaks with each movement. Those muscle fibers, consequently, cannot help growing in size and power at their fastest. Following is revealed the secret of Yogametrics.

How to use Yogametrics to acquire great muscle strength

Everything in Yoga is based upon the control of the mind over the body. In Yogametrics you control the resistance of the muscles of your body with your mind. You simply create a *vivid mental reproduction* of the obstacle you expect your muscles to overcome, and then *go through the effort* of overcoming that obstacle *as if it actually existed.* Here is an example of Yogametrics which you can do right now to develop big arms (triceps) and chest muscles.

1. Lie flat on your back and push upwards with your hands, towards the ceiling, until your arms are fully extended.
2. Bring your hands back down.
3. Create, now, a mental reproduction of the ceiling *as having dropped down intact,* and that you are holding it from crushing you, with your hands, just an inch above your chest.
4. To "save" your life, push with *all your might* against that "ponderously heavy" ceiling. Mentally reproduce the dropped ceiling as *just heavy enough* to compel you to exert full power to push it from you slowly but surely, until your arms are fully extended.

5. Then banish the mental reproduction and let your arms come back down. You will be astonished how hard and bulging they will feel. (Your chest muscles will, too.)

Unusual? Nothing of the kind. Practically every athlete does that regularly in his own sport. Swimmers, runners, walkers, rowers, jumpers, baseball players, acrobats, golfers—all have to exert themselves each time they compete against the same approximate ground resistance, ball resistance, body weight resistance. And yet —their same muscles have to perform *more and more powerfully* each time before they can move faster, jump higher, or hit the ball farther. And they do it regularly and *break their own records time and again!*

How do they do it? The athlete does it by *mentally reproducing* the ground, ball or other obstacle as suddenly offering his muscles *more resistance than it ever did.*

And then the miracle takes place. The muscles opposing his movements (his *antagonist* muscles) immediately tense *reflexly* to brake his performing muscles from dislocating his joints with their sudden, supreme effort. By doing so, though, they increase *their own* resistance to his performing muscles, and thus compel the latter to exert themselves *all the harder.* That's how the athlete breaks his own records, as well as those of others, again and again.

The reason it works so effectively is that, as you are already aware, when you are a novice at any sport, you are awkward and waste energy by doing with difficulty what the expert does effortlessly. Why? Because, when you are a novice you instinctively contract your opposing (your antagonist) muscles strongly against your performing muscles. To become skillful at the sport you have to practice *relaxing* your antagonist muscles when you engage in it, and free your performing muscles from their handicapping and weakening effects and allow them to execute their movements and actions with full leverage and power.

THE SECRET OF YOGAMETRICS

The secret of Yogametrics consists of doing *purposely* what you do as a novice. When you do the simple movement, in other words, *tense* the antagonist muscles hard, thereby compelling your performing muscles to tense *harder still* to overcome the increased resistance to their action. *More* muscle fibers of both sets of muscles will then contract to oppose each other, and both of them will therefore add bulk and power to each other *faster than they could any other way*. As both sets of muscles grow stronger and bigger, just mentally reproduce the obstacle to the performing muscles (the dropped ceiling, say) as getting progressively heavier, and both sets of muscles will continue getting bigger and stronger!

That, in a nutshell, is the secret of Yogametrics for acquiring muscle bulk and muscle power with surprising speed. You can increase the resistance to your performing muscles indefinitely that way and make your muscles grow to herculean proportions. Indeed, you can mentally reproduce the ceiling as so heavy that you can't budge it at all, and compel your muscles fibers to contract to the "popping" point. Not only that, but you can easily position your performing muscles into their best angles of pull when you use them that way, and *then* develop their bulk and power at the speediest pace possible. And you require no weights or contraptions of any kind to help you. All you need are your mental reproductions.

NOTE: *Never* hold your breath when you exercise. Exhale gradually, instead, as you overcome the resistance. Otherwise, you increase the pressure in your abdomen, and that prevents the blood in the veins in the lower part of your body from returning to your lungs and heart. Physiologists, indeed, advise against straining efforts by persons with inherited weak and thin-walled veins. Tight garters, tight belts and straining are equally dangerous. Suspenders are therefore healthier to wear.

You will now put Yogametrics to practical application as follows and develop different big muscles of your body. *Any* simple movement in this book, though, can be used in the Yogametric manner and develop just as fantastically the muscles which they are scientifically perfected to tone up.

How to acquire big, powerful arms and shoulders with Yogametrics with surprising speed

Following are illustrated routines for your guidance in applying the science of Yogametrics.

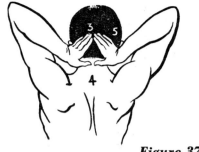

elbows as high
as possible

hands bent upward
at the wrists

Figure 37

top view

shoulder

45°

Figure 38

THE BICEPS BULGE "45" (*Figures 37, 38*).

(The Biceps Bulge 45 encourages muscular growth to its fastest and greatest.)

How to hyper-contract your biceps:

1. Raise both arms straight overhead.
2. Palms facing each other.
3. Flex your elbows, so that your hands come down behind your head   (*Figure 37*).
4. Now, bend your hands as far as possible upwards at the wrists.
5. Turn the thumb-halves of your hands *upwards* to the extreme, supinating the forearms and tightening the biceps into painful balls.
6. At the same time, angle your arms and elbows at 45 degree angles to your shoulders (*Figure 38*).
7. Hold them this way for two seconds.

Frequency

2–4 times a day.

THE BICEPS BULGE "90" (*Figures 39, 40*).

How to hyper-contract the biceps brachii:

1. Raise arms straight out at the sides, to just above shoulder level.
2. Flex the forearm to just beyond a 90 degree angle with the upper arm (*Figure 39*).
3. Turn the hands hard backwards at the wrists (*Figure 40*).
4. Set the arms at 45 degree angles to the shoulders.
5. Turn the thumb-halves of the hands outwards to the extreme, to supinate the forearm to the full and make the biceps hurt like a boil.
6. Maintain the contraction for two seconds.

Frequency

2–4 times a day.

arms above shoulder level

Figure 39

top view

45°

Figure 40

THE PSYCHERGO-TRICEPS, No. 1 (*Figures 41, 42*).

How to do this simple movement (Figure 41).

1. Draw shoulders up.
2. Palms forward, with thumb-halves twisted backwards *hard*.
3. Arms straight, but far apart. Tense them as hard as you can (but keep your palms *open*).
4. Hold contraction for two seconds.

NOTE: At the start, when you draw your shoulders up, rotate them *outwards* and *backwards* (*Figure 42*).

This simple movement contracts your triceps so powerfully that they cramp quickly.

Frequency

1–5 times a day. Develops tremendously the inner (long) head of triceps.

THE PSYCHERGO-TRICEPS, No. 2 (*Figures 43, 44, 45*).

1. Turn the palms backwards. (*Figures 43, 44*). Then outwards. (*Figure 45*).
2. Draw up the shoulders. Arms straight. (*Figures 43, 44*).
3. Tense hard.

Develops: Lateral (outer) head of triceps.

Frequency

1–5 times a day.

THE ANTERIOR SHOULDER WING (*Figures 46, 47*).

1. Sit relaxed in a chair,
2. With arms at sides (*Figure 46*).

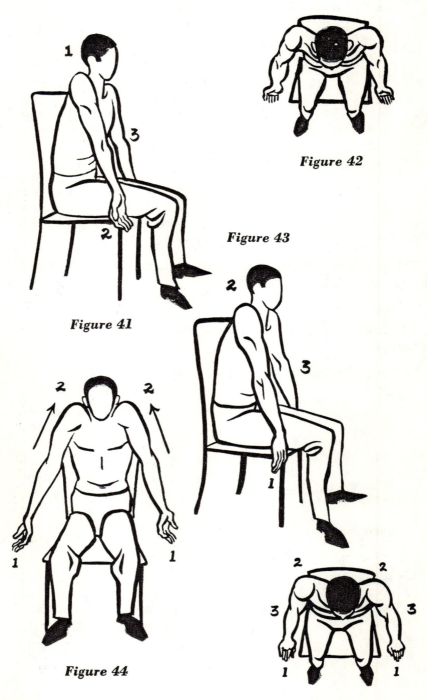

Figure 42

Figure 43

Figure 41

Figure 44

Figure 45

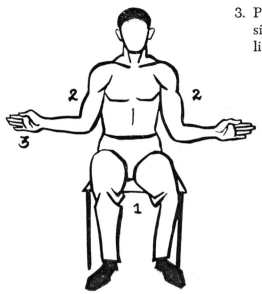

3. Point lower arms out at sides, almost on a straight line with body.

4. Now, move both arms, like hooks, till upper arms are about 45 degrees to body. (*Figure 47*).

Figure 46

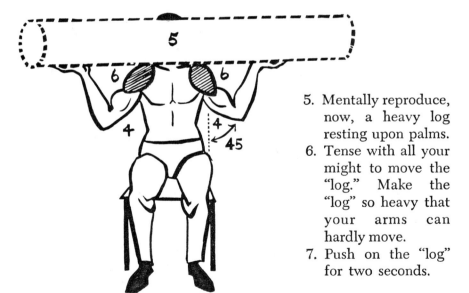

5. Mentally reproduce, now, a heavy log resting upon palms.
6. Tense with all your might to move the "log." Make the "log" so heavy that your arms can hardly move.
7. Push on the "log" for two seconds.

Figure 47

Frequency

2 times a day. Your front shoulder muscles (your deltoids) will fairly pop right through your skin.

THE LATERAL SHOULDER WING (*Figures 48, 49*).

1. Sit relaxed in a chair.
2. Point lower arms forward at sides, at right angles to the body (*Figure 48*).
3. Now (*Figure 49*), move both arms, like hooks, *outwards*, till they are just above the level of your shoulders.
4. Mentally reproduce, now, a heavy "log" resting across your shoulders.
5. Tense with all your might to move the "log." Make the "log" so heavy that your arms can hardly move.
6. Push up on the "log" for two seconds.

Figure 48

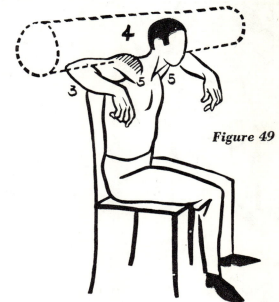

Figure 49

Frequency

2 times a day. Your shoulder muscles on top, will fairly pop through your skin.

NOTE: Do *not* exercise for about two and one-half hours after a heavy meal. Aside from the possibilities of causing indigestion, exercising after a meal adds a considerable load to the work of your heart. During digestion, the blood flow through your heart is increased over 80 percent, and during strenuous work it is increased by about 400 percent.

Also note that everybody's muscles do not enlarge to the same size, no matter what exercises they do. The muscles of a long-limbed person do not thicken as much as those of a short-limbed person, because the increased bulk within his muscle fibers has more room to spread out lengthwise than that of the short-limbed person, and so his gain in muscle girth is less obvious.

Even if you don't seek a big, powerful physique, though, you should still do these Yogametric exercises to a limited degree to build up strikingly hard, strong muscles. You should because your body musculature constitutes 43 percent of your body weight. Your body musculature contains more than one-third of all your body proteins, and contributes about one-half of the metabolic activity of your resting body. It also holds a tremendous amount of body heat and can keep you warmer in cold weather. When your muscles are neglected, besides, they not only atrophy, but degenerate into permanent fat.

Case histories

How 39-Year-Old Fred Used Yogametrics to Improve His Shape Greatly in a Few Weeks

Fred, 39 years old, was sick of seeing his misshapen body in the bathroom mirror every day. He was six feet tall, but weighed only 145 pounds. His arms were like pipestems; his chest described a concave curve from neck to waist; his shoulders sloped like the sides of a pyramid and dragged his back down with them, so that it humped, unless he forcibly stood straight. His legs had a weak, wishy-washy feeling, like jelly. His whole body felt strangely relaxed, as if he had just soaked 20 minutes in a bathtub full of hot water.

I taught Fred how to use Yogametrics for his torso, arms and legs, as well as dynamic, diaphragm piston-powering. *The very next day* he already experienced a delightful firming in his chest, arms, shoulders and legs. He was not yet firm, of course, but he was feeling as if he were. That filled him with such a feverish enthusiasm that his whole attitude towards his body changed practically overnight, and he saw himself as a sturdy, rugged, virile man. Within a few short weeks he added enough size and muscle-tone to his body to look impressive in the mirror. His shoulders appeared amazingly broader to the eye, too, because they sloped noticeably less, and therefore extended sideways more prominently. His upper arm had grown over an inch, and his chest nearly two inches. And Fred had spent only eight minutes a day at it.

How 42-Year-Old Cliff, Using Yogametrics, Competed in a Physique Contest Against Weight-Lifters and Body-Builders Half His Age

Cliff was a married man of 41. He was inspired by the physiques of the muscle men he saw in pictures and on the beach, and wished to look like them. "But I'm too old," he told me regretfully.

"You are not!" I assured him, and I urged him to try Yoga metrics.

Cliff did the Yogametric exercises faithfully five times a week, up to one hour, or more, each time. (Title-holding body builders spend from three to five hours working out daily, five times or more a week. Some, in fact, spend 35 hours *or more* working out a week, and they are practically all young men in their early twenties.) Cliff's improvement was so astonishing that even the young body builders on the beach persuaded him to compete in the local physique contests. He did so twice against my advice, but was not ready for them and failed to place.

Then Cliff trained for months without competing, and prepared himself for the big local contest—the one to select a winner to compete for Mr. America. He was barely shaded out of third place—against a winner who was soon Mr. America and Mr. Universe!

At 42, Cliff had achieved his amazing feat with Yogametrics alone, one hour a day, while the winner had spent up to eight hours daily at the weights for the last three months before the contest, even though he had already gathered a long list of trophies during the years before that. Today, as he nears 60, Cliff still looks almost as good as he did then, on only 15 minutes a day, three times a week.

Summary of the steps for using Yoga secrets for big powerful muscles

In order to apply Yoga secrets for big, powerful muscles, you have to counteract the wear-and-tear of the four horsemen of the mastabah on your spinal disks, and develop your muscles with Yogametrics. You do so by:

1. Avoiding exercises (like weight-lifting) which add abnormally to the pressure exerted upon your spinal disks, as well as isometric contractions, which temporarily obstruct your blood circulation, threaten your heart, and may cause blood clots. Rely instead on
2. Using the best angle of pull of the muscle, and
3. On mental reproduction, and on
4. Increasing the resistance of the antagonist muscles to make your muscles grow stronger most quickly.

With these Yogametric secrets you will activate the greatest number of your muscle fibers at one time when you body build, and force them to grow faster than they could otherwise. With them you will also increase your muscle power fastest, because you can make their resistance to your muscles as strong as you want with mental reproduction, any time you wish. And they are always *safe* to use, because you can halt any movement *any time* you wish. You require absolutely no apparatus, weights or external resistance of any kind. Most important, you can do it anywhere, at any age.

Yoga
Secrets
for More   10
Sex Power

The asceticism of the Yogi withdraws him from active participation in sex. That does not mean, though, that the Yogi is impotent. On the contrary, cases of Yogis who have returned to the material life and mated have revealed them to have sex powers at ages far beyond the common age of the male climacteric. That is not surprising, because the Yogi considers his sexual potency as one of the main sources of his extraordinary energy, muscle power, disease resistance, physical endurance and longevity. He insists that Western man is deficient in all these qualities because he does not know how to intensify and prolong his natural, inborn sex power. For thousands of years, much of the Yogi's efforts have been expended in that direction, and so he is a true expert. His secrets of sex power have therefore been carefully studied and refined for *your own use* in the practical Western world, to enable you to gain the utmost benefit from them as quickly as possible, without subjecting yourself to his rigid routines. The case histories at the end of the chapter prove how effective they can be for you.

**Your semergy: the natural sex energy which your body
stores within you, and how its loss weakens
the powers of your mind and body**

A vast amount of natural energy is stored within you in the form of sex energy. The Yogis practice asceticism (sex abstinence)

122

in order to harness it and use it for other purposes in their bodies. You are familiar with the muscle fatigue that possesses you following the orgasm, despite the glandular stimulation you then enjoy. And it is frequently succeeded by vague neuralgic sensations and even with fasciculations (short jumping of your thigh muscles). Although an occasional athlete claims to feel at his best for competition immediately after sexual indulgence, the great majority of them claim just the opposite. The great majority of them, indeed,. confess to suffering from a sensation of "jelly-like relaxation" all over and to have lost the "solid, all-over feeling" they had before. Such a loss may be due partly to the emotional shock of the orgasm, and to the consequent temporary exhaustion of the nervous system. But it is also due, as the Yogis insist, to the temporary depletion of certain glandular secretions of the body and their energy-filled contents (your semergy). You will readily understand what the Yogis mean by that when you study the composition of human semen.

The Composition of Human Semen

The liquid bulk of semen consists of a mixture of the secretions of a variety of gland and inner body tubes. Its calcium, urea and sugar contents are twice as high as they are in blood. Its sugar, too, is the easily available fructose, rather than the more difficultly available glucose. Its spermatozoa are composed largely of nucleoproteins, which are an important constituent of the nucleus of the body cell. It also contains large amounts of inorganic phosphorous. These and the fructose are synthesized in the seminal vessels.

During ejaculation, a greatly increased amount of all these parts of the semen are poured out around the swimming spermatozoa.

The resulting loss of nucleoproteins (since your sperm itself is composed of it) causes an urgent call for more from your body, and your nervous system is forced to surrender some of its own to meet it. But since the nucleoprotein content of nerve tissue is low, the metabolism of your nerve cell and the nutrition of the nerve are both decreased on account of that, and that lowers your body metabolism and the Spino-Volt of your nerves. The messages which your nerves carry from your body to your brain, and the commands which they deliver from your brain to your body, therefore, are weakened, slowed down and altered. And so, the natural control of your conscious and subconscious minds over your body lessens. Your physical strength and energy also decrease. That's how your loss of semergy weakens the powers of your mind and body.

How the four horsemen of the mastabah reduce your natural, inborn sex power

The four horsemen reduce your natural, inborn sex power by:

1. Impairing the normal functioning of your hypothalamus.
2. Oppressing you with a body sag.

You will now be shown how the four horsemen bring on those unwanted changes in you and reduce your natural, inborn sex power, and how the refined, scientifically-perfected Yoga secrets counteract them and recharge you.

How the four horsemen reduce your natural, inborn sex power by impairing your hypothalamus

Your natural, inborn sex power consists not only of your semergy, but also of your general, all-over muscle tone, as well as of the natural, instinctive sex psychology which you possessed before the social customs repressed and disciplined it. Fear, doubt, pessimism and feelings of inferiority, and even of sexual hostility, then superimposed themselves upon your daily experiences and reduced your natural, inborn, instinctive sex psychology. Over the years, too, the four horsemen reduced it further still, as you will see, until you retained but a sample of your original inborn sex power.

The four horsemen reduced it significantly by jamming your head down upon your neck, and by dragging your shoulders, your rib-box and your spine, downwards. That narrowed the vertebral openings of the spinal nerves that supply your sex glands and organs, and lessened the nerve-electricity (the Spino-Volt) which the blood vessels to your sex glands and organs received from your hypothalamus (in your brain). That, in turn, diminished the amount of blood which the blood vessels brought to your sex glands and organs, thereby reducing the natural metabolism and physiological functions of your sex glands and organs (*Figure 50*). Your natural, inborn sex power becomes then

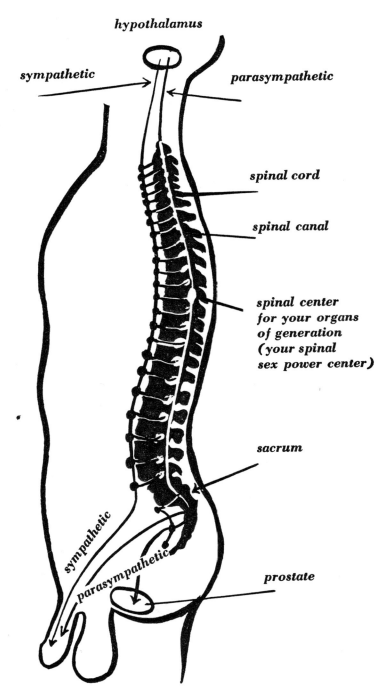

Figure 50
Nerve Supply to Your Organs of Generation

obviously less than it would be, and the *physiological awareness of that fact is flashed back to your hypothalamus.*

The normal functioning of your hypothalamus itself, besides, is also impaired by the narrowed vertebral openings of your upper back, because one of these happens to squeeze the sympathetic nerve which controls the blood vessels to your hypothalamus. That narrows these blood vessels and therefore diminishes the blood supply to your hypothalamus. Your natural, inborn sexual aggressiveness is, as a result, reduced still more.

Messages of this fact are flashed to your conscious mind, and your conscious mind immediately delivers a *still weaker* command to your sex organs to respond to stimulation. The vicious circle repeats itself again and again in that manner and lessens your natural, inborn sex power more and more.

How to regain lost, natural, inborn sex power by restoring more of the normal functioning of your hypothalamus

In order to regain lost, natural, inborn sex power, you have to knead and flexibilitate" your upper and lower back. By doing so, you stimulate both your sympathetic and your parasympathetic nervous systems, and both are intimately involved in your sex power. Your sex stimulus is ruled by your sympathetics (your

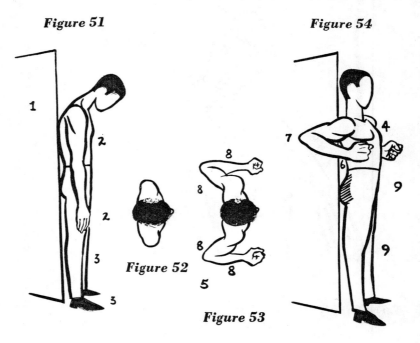

Figure 51

Figure 54

Figure 52

Figure 53

fighting nerves), for it fills you with the desire to conquer and possess. But your parasympathetics (your loving nerves) then stimulate your prostate to secrete. The orgasm, finally, is ruled by your sympathetics, because the testicles and their secretions are under the control of aggressive emotions. The ideal Yoga move-ment for regaining lost, natural sex power is the Yoga Sex Power Invigorator (*Figures 51–57*).

THE YOGA SEX POWER INVIGORATOR

The position to assume (Figure 51).

1. Stand relaxed against the free end of an opened door, or against the corner of a doorway, with
2. Shoulders and arms drooping, relaxed.
3. Feet hip-width apart. Legs straight, but relaxed.
4. Inhale (*Figure 52*),
5. Clench fists,
6. Arch your back,
7. Bend your arms, and draw them far back.
8. Now, forearms are parallel to each other (*Figure 53*). Shoulders are drawn backwards.
9. Hips flexed hard, knees straight (*Figure 52*).

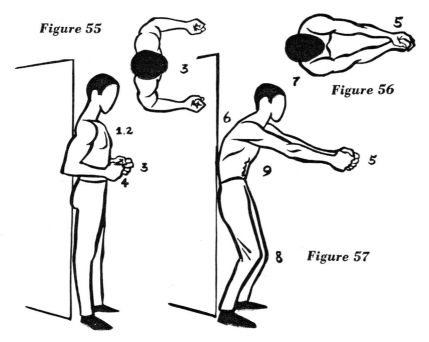

Figure 55

Figure 56

Figure 57

How to do this simple movement (Figures 54–57).

1. Start exhaling (*Figure 54*),
2. Curving your back, and
3. Driving both fists straight forward, about the level of your waist (*Figures 54–55*).
4. Start contracting your abdominal muscles.

Now, turn to Figures 56 and 57.

5. Drive arms straight out until they meet. At the same time:
6. Round your back.
7. Round your shoulders forward.
8. Bend knees (*Figure 56*), and
9. Contract abdominals hard, and exhale all the way out.

This simple movement

1. Stimulates your sympathetics (upper back).
2. Stimulates your parasympathetics (lower back).
3. And develops, to a degree, all the important abdominal muscles: the rectus abdominis, external and internal obliques, and the transversalis.

Frequency

5–10 times every morning.

Do it vigorously, too, in order to stimulate your sex power Spino-Volt. Draw arms back hard, and develop back, also. Peps you up by starting the blood flowing faster back to your heart. Inhale deeply, besides, and enlarge your rib-box.

How your body sag reduces your natural, inborn sex power

Body sag (that is, a sagging or protruding abdomen) is a common cause of low-back strain resulting from the relentless traumas of the four horsemen. The weight, and the downward-forward pull, of your protruding abdomen, fatigues your abdominal muscles, as well as increases the merciless downward-stretching of gravity on the weary ligaments supporting your lower back. Your low-back curve, for that reason, deepens and throws more torso-weight upon the joints of the tail-halves of its vertebrae. And so, you experience vague pains across your lower back, which are worse at the end of the day. If ignored because no clinical symptoms are apparent, it can progress to the stage where it may compress the spinal nerves of your lower back hard enough, and your urine, upon analysis, may occasionally show evidence of incipient diabetes, and of heart-kidney disturbances. And yet, you do not have a fat belly, for if you suddenly assume correct posture by drawing in your chin enough and raising your chest, your abdomen is promptly drawn into place, and the size of your waist is shrunken by several inches. The moment you relax, though, your torso drops back into the body sag and resumes the abnormal strains which it places on the spinal nerves of your lower back.

There are several reasons why your body sag reduces your natural, inborn sex power. First, the increased inner curving of your lower back, narrows excessively the vertebral openings in it, and those *are the very ones* which are handicapped because they possess the least extra space, and yet the biggest spinal nerves do pass through them. Secondly, the sympathetic nerves, which control the blood supply of your sex glands, also pass through those excessively narrowed vertebral openings. When this blood supply is reduced, the nourishment to your sex glands is reduced, and your semergy is also consequently reduced. The message-carrying nerves of your sex glands then flash less sex drive to your conscious and subconscious minds, and that lessens your natural, inborn, psychological, sex power. The vicious circle repeats itself until your natural, inborn sex power is shrunken to a shadow of itself.

If your body sag is due to obesity, the weight of your heavy abdomen will bring about similar dire results. Wearing tight clothing at your waist or neck can contribute to body sag by slowing down the return of the blood from your legs to your lungs and heart, and thereby weakening the muscles of your lower back by diminishing their normal blood supply. The jar and strain of training or competing in different sports, as well as your wearing shoes with higher heels, may deepen the inner curve of your lower back by throwing your hips farther back, and then balancing their malposition by throwing your upper back further backwards, too. Accidents, blows, occupation, and a "pot" belly may all lead to body sag and weaken your natural, inborn sex power. These and many other causes may contribute to body sag and reduce your sex power. It is most important for you to eliminate your body sag, then, so as to regain lost natural, inborn

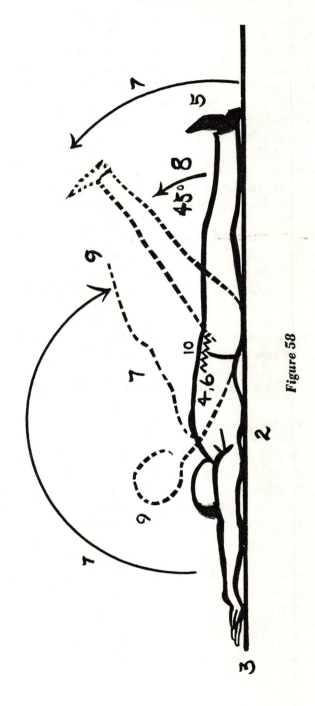

Figure 58

sex power. So, do regularly the Abdominal Double Curl, the simple movement which the Yogi originated, and which is here scientifically perfected (*Figure 58*).

THE ABDOMINAL DOUBLE CURL—TO REDUCE YOUR BODY SAG—AND RESTORE YOUR NATURAL, INBORN SEX VIGOR

The position to assume (Figure 58)

1. Lie flat on your bed, or on a softened floor. Do not lie on the hard, bare floor.
2. Lie on your back.
3. Stretch arms out directly in back of your head.

How to do this simple movement

4. Inhale deeply.
5. Curl your toes towards your head.
6. Now, gather your strength and *exhale* as you
7. Raise your arms and legs at the same time.
8. Raise your legs no higher than 45 degrees from the ground.
9. Raise your body as you bring your arms forwards and downwards, as if trying to touch your toes with your fingers.
10. Relax and repeat.

This simple movement develops (Figure 58–10):

●1. Rectus abdominis. (The horizontal grooves across the front of your waist.)
2. External and internal obliques (the muscles of the fronts and sides of your waist).

Frequency

3–5 times a day.

●This is perhaps the greatest abdominal "shrinker" of them all. It is hard to do, but it works miracles for your waistline, stomach, circulation and heart, for it makes it beat fast almost immediately. Making your heart beat fast once a day is one sure way to keep the fat off it.

Make this simple movement a regular routine for the rest of your life for a strikingly masculine appearance.

How to eat to regain and retain lost natural, inborn sex power

Eating heavy foods which are slow to digest and which saddle you with oppressive discomfort for hours after consuming them will surely devitalize your sex power, not only for hours, but even for days afterwards, because such foods are likely to produce frustrating gas attacks and constipation. Such heavy foods include fried foods, foods with high concentrations of saturated fats (fatty meats, brazil nuts, cocoanut, avocado, cream and cream products, pastries, *un*-skimmed milk, and such products).

Unsaturated fats, on the other hand, such as those found in walnuts, are absolutely essential in the metabolism of your body because they possess a high energy component which is capable of large storage. This high energy is vitally necessary for maximum sex power. For protein, eat lean meats. Salt-water fish, though, is still better because it contains very little saturated fat; while even the lean meats contain an alarming quantity of invisible saturated fat. Protein is necessary because it will maintain your normal blood volume by drawing excessive fluid from your tissue fluids into your blood vessels. But, limit your fat deposits (for they will cause body sag and reduce your sex power) by avoiding foods containing saturated fats, or containing *excessive* amounts of carbohydrates (sugar), or excessive proteins.

Last, but not least, drink enough water every day to produce your normal volume of digestive juices, for these amount to at least two quarts a day. Water also importantly avoids intestinal autointoxication, which is a primary cause of reduced sex power. This is so because the intestinal autointoxication causes constipation, and the resulting hard fecal matter presses down for days at a time, in your lower and sigmoid colons, against your prostate, thus exhausting your sex drive.

How Yogametric deep knee-bends safely recharge you with renewed sex power

Yogametric deep knee-bends are the effective means for flushing your sex glands with blood and stimulating the renewed synthesis of semergy. They also constitute the safe and easy way to increase the power of your thighs and hips—a power that fills you with a feeling of greatly increased sex power, for your thighs and hips are most important for the pelvic thrust. That feeling, in turn, is flashed to your conscious and subconscious minds, and these at once regain their natural, inborn psychological sex power and command your sex organs and glands to conquer all.

Deep knee-bends with weights, though, are not safe for your back and they are not recommended for the average case.

Yogametric deep knee-bends are free from dangers possible when using weights. And since you require no weights or apparatus for doing them, you can do them anywhere, any time of day, even when you travel. So, use the *Psychergo Squat* (hardly changed from the original Yoga version), for bringing back and "recharging" your natural, inborn sex power.

THE PSYCHERGO SQUAT

The position to assume (Figures 59, 60).

1. Sit at the edge of the Yogi Bench, or of something equally low.
2. Your feet and knees comfortably relaxed and apart. (Heels about 14 inches apart.)
3. Drop your head between your knees, and
4. Hook your forearms under about the middle of your thighs.

How to do this simple movement (Figure 61).

5. Keep your forearms hooked under your thighs, and
6. Straighten your knees by pulling your thighs up powererfully with your thigh-hooked forearms. BUT
7. *Resist* their straightening with your thighs. Your thigh muscles will contract tremendously.

This simple movement achieves (Figure 62):

8. Develops fast the *front* and side muscles of your thighs, as well as shakes loose any fat on them.
9. Wears fat off your hips because it *stretches*, rather than contracts, their muscles. Therefore, also keeps them small by not enlarging their muscles with unnecessary bulk.
10. Flushes your gonads with nutritive blood because it opens wide the vertebral openings of your lower vertebral joints.

Frequency

2 times a day. (If you do it with much weaker pulling and resisting, you can do it faster, up to 10 times a day.)

Figure 59

Figure 60

Figure 61

Figure 62

Case histories

HOW HARRY REGAINED HIS LOST MALE AUTHORITY IN HIS HOME

Harry was known as a typical good-provider type of husband. He was no standout anywhere, but he was dependable, conscientious and hard-working and dutifully brought his paycheck home to his wife, Ava, to spend as she thought best. Ava was not just spending it; she was wasting it on needless and extravagant expenditures, as if Harry were made of money. Naturally, this worried him.

Several times he tried to discuss the matter with Ava, but she just returned him an impatient look and snatched up a fashion magazine and buried her nose in it. So, Harry had to remain silent and let Ava continue wasting his paycheck unnecessarily, week after week.

Harry confided his problem in me. One look at him and I realized that he exerted little authority over his headstrong wife. Not only was he flabby and pusillaminous in appearance and manner, but there was no longer anything about him that suggested a master "he-man." Even his walk was an apologetic shuffle. He admitted that his romantic life with Ava was practically nil, for her main concern seemed to be constantly to buy clothes and other things for herself. She spent her time with similar female friends during the day and threw lavish parties for them and their husbands on weekends: parties in which he himself was little more than a figurehead.

I taught Harry how to do the Abdominal Double Curl and the Yoga Sex Power Invigorator, but he confessed that Ava never would let him exercise at home. Whenever he had tried to, she had scoffed at him and ordered him to "get your exercise doing something worthwhile around here, like repairing the house, painting the kitchen, polishing the car, mowing the lawn." To his great relief, I reassured him that he could do these secret Yogametric movements right at work, during his coffee-break, or even in his bathroom at home without Ava suspecting what he was about, since they would take up so little time.

In less than two weeks Harry had tightened up his loose waist noticeably. His thighs felt springy, too, and added already a healthy aggressiveness to his walk and posture. For once, he said, he felt more like the man he was born to be. Indeed, he confessed, women who had ignored him before "like the paper on the wall," were looking at him now! All these changes filled his mind with a steadily growing sex pride in himself.

Harry then tackled Ava again on the extravagance question. When she thwarted him, his new manly aggressiveness and driving capacity caught her unawares. *Within a couple of weeks Harry was the much-cherished master of his home!*

How rundown, 58-year-old Vincent
won for himself a 32-year-old wife

At 53 Vincent had been suddenly widowed. His children were grown up and married, and Vincent felt as if the whole world had caved in on him. So he sold the home and rented a small apartment, for the house was too big for himself alone. But his misery only increased. Vincent was not used to living alone, especially after enjoying an ideal marriage. He missed those delicious, home-cooked meals and family discussions.

A few years later, at 58, Vincent was close to being a physical wreck and, in a way, a mental wreck. He had degenerated into a steady drinker, suffered from stomach ulcers, underwent a serious operation, and experienced vague, mysterious pains in his back which occasionally grew so intense that they drove him to the doctor. Nothing significant showed up on the X-ray film, though, except the usual physiological and pathological changes common at Vincent's age; that is, a degree of spinal disk hardening and wear-and-tear, a degree of narrowing of his vertebral openings, a degree of misshapening of his vertebral bodies, and the usual increase in the depths of the wrong-curves in his spine. None required urgent medical care.

Then, one day, Vincent saw a new employee in the firm, a woman, a minor executive of about 32. Her name was Lana. She did not resemble his dead wife much in appearance, but her personality seemed like her duplicate. To Vincent it was as if his wife had returned to him, but in a different physical form. He was so completely overcome that he could hardly wait to talk to Lana. She replied kindly, but it was obvious that she detected the pitiable wreck that he was. And so, he faded away from her vicinity, his body feeling completely toneless.

As Vincent watched her gracefully walking through the premises later, her comparatively young body so firm, he realized with a desperate sigh what a pathetic carcass he had become, and how little he could offer her if he could be so unbelievably lucky as to marry her.

Marry her! The very idea was too ludicrous for words.

When he confessed to me, I disagreed with him that he had no chance whatsoever with Lana, and reminded him of the significant number of women who regularly married men much older than they, and who seemed to live happily thereafter.

"But not a living corpse like me!" he scoffed back.

"Don't be so sure!" I corrected him.

I showed him how to do all the Yogametric simple movements for sex power. He felt so much better after doing them *the very first time* that he continued doing them eagerly, determined to become the man he would have still been, had he *not* lost his wife. His body sag lessened, and his thighs hardened so steadily that he soon was arising from a chair after sitting, not like a weary old man on his last legs, but more like an active youth bounding to his feet, ready to take part in something exciting. Vincent felt younger and younger every day. When he encountered the 32-year-old Lana, instead of still feeling like a shameful cast-off, he now joked with her. Her return gaze, too, he admitted, was losing that distant, respect-for-age wall it had built between them.

"I am *dreaming* of her now!" he confessed to me after less than six weeks of Yogametrics. "And they are romantic dreams!"

Vincent changed so fast after that, that he soon took Lana out to dinner. Thereafter he changed like a miracle. Within a year they were married. Before another year passed, Vincent was the proud father of a bounding eight pound boy! "I feel again like I'm 35!" he exclaimed, rushing in to hand out the cigars. "Those Yogis sure pumped my manhood back into me!"

With Yoga for sex power, desperately rundown, 58-year-old Vincent had won for himself a most attractive 32-year-old woman for a wife by recharging himself as I guided him.

Summary steps for using the secrets of Yoga for sex power

To acquire Yoga for sex power and recharge yourself with its natural physical and mental stimulations, you have to:

1. Regain the normal functions of your hypothalamus.
2. Reduce your body sag and its resulting discomforts which irritate your conscious and subconscious minds.
3. Eat foods which do not saddle you with discomfort afterwards.
4. Do Yogametric deep knee-bends.

These routines will arouse your latent psychological sex power, and that will increase the Spino-Volt to your sex glands and, of course, your sex power.

Yoga Secrets for Personal Popularity

11

As incredible as it might seem at first, the Yogi had urgent reasons for developing an unmatched power of popularity. Being a hermit, first of all, he had no friends, particularly when he journeyed. Secondly, he encountered hostile persons or groups constantly, either in the wilderness, or when he passed by, or through, strange villages, which he regularly did. He usually chose suitable hills to dwell on, too, and these, for the most part, belonged to landlords of power and authority, who could send their servants to chase him off at any time. The Yogi's only hope for safety lay in making himself so fascinating to all such people that he was left unmolested, or even saved from extermination.

The fact that he managed to exist so long in the midst of all these personal perils proved that he was deeply liked, although he hardly said a word or made a move to make himself popular. Considering how raggedly attired he was most of the time, how little his pursuits were respected by the people at large, and how little he contributed to the material welfare of the community, he must have mastered the greatest secrets of popularity imaginable. Those well-guarded secrets have now been carefully studied and refined for *your own use* in the Western world, to enable you to gain the utmost benefit from them as quickly as possible without

138

subjecting yourself to exhausting disciplines. The case histories prove how effective they can be for you.

How the four horsemen reduce your natural, inborn power of popularity

The four horsemen of the mastabah reduce your natural, inborn power of popularity by:

1. Distorting your body.
2. Tightening your muscles by bringing on subchronic lumbago, subchronic rheumatism, uneven muscular development or any other related subchronic conditions in you which cause muscle strain.
3. Abnormal positions maintained regularly, such as through faulty posture or in your occupation.
4. Causing devitalizing, subchronic aches and pains arising from subclinical (unfelt) pressure on your spinal nerves.
5. Decreasing your natural, inborn nerve tone.
6. Forming popularity-undermining frowns and wrinkles on your face.

You will now be shown how those unwanted changes take place in you and reduce your natural, inborn power of popularity, and also the refined, scientifically-perfected Yoga secrets for counteracting them and acquiring popularity swiftly.

How the four horsemen distort your body and steadily reduce your natural, inborn power of popularity

Due to the two-legged position, the constant downpull of gravity upon the spine in the vertical position will force wrong-back curves into the spine of even the strongest and healthiest person alive. This occurs because the correct human posture, unlike that of the four-footed animal, is not part of its natural inheritance, but has to be *learned*. In order to maintain the unnatural, upright position, you have to expend more energy constantly than you would have to otherwise. Indeed, you have to *waste* energy. It is believed, as a matter of fact, that *one-third* of your energy is used to maintain your upright position alone! If you weigh 200 pounds, in other words, you actually carry 266 pounds of body weight around! It is just as if you were constantly moving around wearing a suit-of-armor weighing 66 pounds. Just imagine how fatigued you'd be from the extra energy dissipated! Look how much more tired you feel when just wearing a heavy overcoat for any length of time, than when you just wear a T-shirt! In the four-footed position you would *save* that wasted energy daily, just as you save the energy of carrying your body around when you lie down flat on your back.

In the two-legged position, though, your body has greater mobility! But to compensate for that, your muscles and ligaments have to work that much harder to keep your body steady. The result of that additional stress and strain is that you suffer from chronic muscular fatigue. Your spine is then left susceptible to wrong-back curves; your body structures fall out of their right places in your body, and you acquire postural defects. These bring on imbalancing muscle spasms as you still try to maintain your body upright, and so your faulty posture grows worse.

On top of that, add the abnormal or unusual positions which you are compelled to assume by your habits or occupation, and you develop faulty body mechanics with resulting limited, re-stricted, hampered and vague painful movements of your spine and hips. You might even suffer additional unbalancing muscle spasms due to occupational exposure to cold, dampness, or alter-nating radical changes in temperature, as the butcher does.

Your troubles are really beginning now, for your faulty posture pulls upon the tough, fibrous sheaths covering the muscles that engirdle your torso and limits the free movements of your lungs when you breathe. Your heart, being pulled downwards by your consequently dropped diaphragm, is elongated and twisted, ren-dering its normal beat difficult, and even instigating mysterious irregularities in the rhythm of its beat.

So, every day, no matter how normal your back is, the steady pounding of the four horsemen will distort it with wrong curves before the day is over. Sleep reduces those wrong-back curves. In time, however, the shapes of your vertebrae and of your spinal disks are altered irreversibly by the relentless trauma incurred, and your wrong-back curves are made increasingly permanent.

How muscle strain reduces your natural, inborn power of popularity

Tight muscles, particularly those on the chest or back, resulting from the traumas discussed above, tend to pull the parts of the body to which they are attached, out of line. Also, muscles that are weak or over-relaxed, allow the parts of the body to which they are attached to deviate out of line through lack of muscular support. If your chest muscles are too tight on your right side, for example, they will round-shoulder your right shoulder, as well as pull your spine, and twist the vertebrae of the resulting wrong-back curve, towards the right and narrow their vertebral openings. If your chest muscles are stronger or tighter than your back muscles, they will round both your shoulders and your torso-back (kyphosis), as well as plague you with burning pains in the middle of your upper back, where your stretched out back muscles are stretched the most thin. Your stomach, liver, spleen, kidneys and your other visceral organs will then tend to drop, and your back will be rushing on the way to arthritis, fusion, and many other ills.

Uneven muscle contractions, like these, lead to subchronic, milder forms of the conditions which follow prolonged muscle strain of the same type, such as subchronic lumbago, subchronic rheumatism, or other related subchronic conditions. Such conditions most commonly afflict young adults who expose themselves to dampness and drafts during and after exercise, and men are affected three times as frequently as women. But they are also common to the adult of all ages whose muscles are unevenly developed from a round-shouldered posture. Your back muscles are then stretched out thin, but your shoulder and chest muscles are hypercontracted, and so you rather easily acquire a long standing, annoying, faint muscle rheumatism in your shoulders and chest following undue exposure to dampness. When you have a body sag, the muscles in the small of your back are in subchronic spasm, while your abdominal muscles are stretched out thin, and so you rather easily acquire a long-standing, faint, subchronic lumbago upon undue exposure to dampness, which is also more common among men.

Vague pains and tenderness accompany the spasm, with an annoying, even if not always noticed, loss of elasticity of the part suffering from it, with a corresponding amount of disability. It may turn into a full-fledged lumbago or rheumatism when you suddenly engage in strenuous work, such as prolonged muscular strain in heavy industry, or from minor effort after you have kept your lower back still too long, on account of the pain of moving it. As long as your acquired, uneven muscular development remains, you are subject to these conditions and regularly suffer, even if you don't suspect it, from a greater or lesser degree of one of them. *The subchronic vague pains and tenderness which they trigger steadily flash their messages of irritation to your subconscious mind and sneakily but steadily, undermine your confidence, optimism and humor and reduce your natural, inborn power of popularity.*

How to loosen and keep limber the tight muscles which cause muscle strain, and thereby regain lost, natural, inborn power of popularity

THE BACK DRAW

The position to assume (Figure 63).

1. Stand with back rounded,
2. Hips drawn in,
3. Knees bent. Exhale.
4. Hold your fists before you, with forearms parallel to the ground.

How to do this simple movement (Figures 64, 65)

5 Draw your elbows back hard, but parallel to each other. Draw back far (*Figure 65–5*).
6. Draw your fists back in an arc. (*Figure 64–6*).

At the same time:

7. Inhale (*Figure 65*).
8. Straighten your back (*Figure 65–8*).
9. Straighten your knees (*Figure 65–9*).

This simple movement develops muscles (Figure 66):

1. Trapezius (1st section). Top of shoulder.
2. Rhomboids. Middle upper back.
3. Sacrospinalis. Lower back.
4. Teres major. Back, under arm.
5. Posterior deltoid. Back of shoulder.
6. Lower section of latissimus doris. V-shaped lower back.

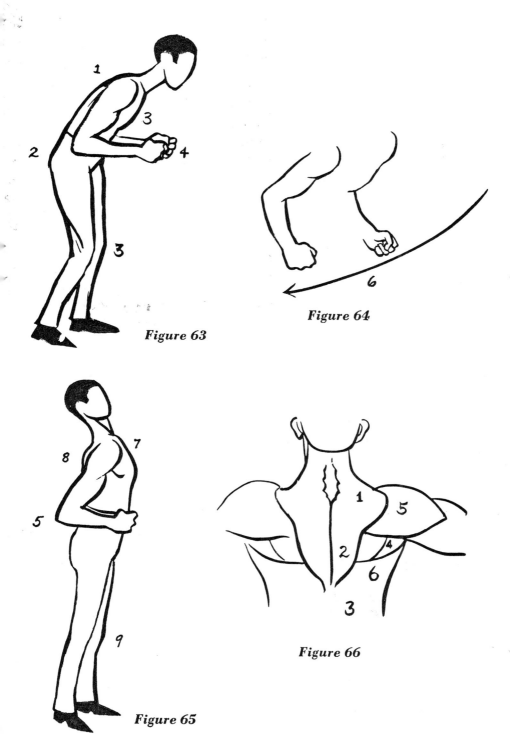

Figure 63

Figure 64

Figure 65

Figure 66

AND, since it also *extends* all these back muscles all the way, with each repetition, it speeds up the blood circulation in them and loosens and limbers them.

If one shoulder or part of your back is less developed than the other, pull back harder with that corresponding arm.

•Don't be misled by the simplicity of this simple movement. It has been worked out to scientific perfection, and enables you to contract your back and posterior shoulder muscles at their best angles of pull.

Frequency

2–5 times a day.

How to relieve the devitalizing subchronic aches and pains arising from subclinical squeezing of your spinal nerves, which steadily reduce your natural, inborn power of popularity

Pain can be relieved by reducing the electric conductivity of the pain-carrying nerve, as by compressing it; or also by cold, drugs (analgesics and narcotics, such as aspirin, morphine, codeine, novocaine), or by reducing the sensitivity of the brain cells which register the pain, as in general anesthesia.

Pain itself, of course, plays an important part in protecting you against the threat of severe disease. In fact, the cure for cancer (Sadove) would be markedly better if the disease would herald its presence by pain in the early stages. The amount of pain one can endure, too, varies from person to person. It depends on the person's temperament, culture, past experience, expectation and fear of danger and, strange as it might seem, on the color of his eyes. The persons most sensitive to pain are those with dark-brown eyes, followed by those with brown, light brown, hazel, green, gray, blue gray, blue. But even those with the same eye color cannot possess the same sensitivity to pain, because their psychological reactions to it varies widely.

Pain, also, tends to grow worse at night, when you have more time to think about it. It grows worse also when something else bothers you. That's why noise, which is a form of pain, has been used to reduce sensitivity to an original pain. (It divides the attention.) Clenching the fists, wringing the hands or gripping a metal bar, also help for that reason. Indeed, that's why soldiers often do not feel their wounds on the battlefield, and why boxers regularly fight on with broken hands but wince the next day when the injury is touched lightly.

Scientists have found that pain reaches its most excruciating point when the skin temperature reaches 152 degrees. The torture of the pain remains constant after that, no matter how much heat is added. Pain past a certain point, it seems, apparently destroys the pain-carrying nerve fibers.

NOTE: A grease burn causes the greatest pain. Next to it are labor pains during childbirth, passing of a large kidney stone, and holding a burning cigarette against the skin. In the next category are heart attacks, muscle cramps, some headaches and facial neuralgia.

Any kind of pain, though, is devitalizing. Even subchronic pain is devitalizing, although it is unfelt or unsuspected, because it lasts so long. It is therefore necessary to relieve it to prevent it from steadily reducing your natural, inborn power of popularity.

How nerve-tone increases your natural, inborn power of popularity

The stronger your Spino-Volt (your spinal cord voltage), the more superior you are mentally, physically and physiologically. The ultimate value of the influence of your nervous system on you lies in the fact that it adds efficiency to the reactions of your muscles (the muscles of your skeleton, as well as the muscles of your different organs and blood vessels) and of your glands. But it cannot do that for you without nerve-tone. Opening your vertebral openings wider *will* increase your nerve-tone more nearly to that of your natural, inborn state. Without Yoga, though, *that will still not be* the best nerve-tone you can regain.

Why? When you stand up after a long confinement in bed, for instance, the muscles of your abdomen and limbs are weak, and the tone of the sympathetic nerves controlling the muscles of the walls of their blood-supplying arteries is lessened. These arteries, for that reason, lack the driving power to pump the blood in your abdomen and lower limbs back into your lungs and heart against the relentless downpull of gravity. Your heart, as a consequence, does not receive enough blood back from your body to enable it to continue pumping out enough of it to maintain normal blood circulation. And so, your blood pressure falls, and the blood flow to your brain becomes inadequate. Due to the resulting less oxygen in your brain, you turn pale, sweat freely, feel giddy or nauseated and faint.

You feel much like that when you suddenly arise after a long sleep. Since your muscle commanding nerves, as well as your sympathetics (your fighting nerves) have not been used strongly for some time, they have lost their tone. Without enough nerve-tone, your natural, inborn power of popularity is considerably reduced, because then you lack even the energy to smile spontaneously, much less to remain pleasant afterwards. So, do the simple Yogatone movements to develop nerve-tone as described below.

How to relieve popularity-decreasing neuralgia with the Yoga oblique nerve-tone

In order to trigger more nerve-tone in a nerve, you have to stretch that nerve. In surgery, nerve-stretching is an operation of forcibly extending or stretching a nerve-trunk. It is resorted to in the treatment of obstinate neuralgia (nerve pain). With the Yoga oblique nerve-tone, of course, you don't stretch the nerve long or permanently and rid it of valuable transmitting qualities; you just rid it of them temporarily with a minor stretching. By doing so, though, you increase the blood circulation through the nerve, cast off its fatigue, stimulate and refresh it, and thereby increase its nerve-tone. The nerve responds faster to stimulation then and transmits messages from your body to your brain, and commands from your brain to your body, more swiftly and intensely. That peps you up and, obviously, adds immeasurably to your decreased natural power of popularity.

The most effective Yogatone simple movement for nerve-stretching, is the right and left Yoga oblique nerve-tone. The abdominal obliques are the muscles on the sides of your waist (*Figure 69*). They are the stabilizers of your rib cage, enabling it to swing, or to be fixed sideways, whenever you move. They also massage your solar plexus, draw the vertebrae of your lower back further apart, and stretch the lower half of your spinal cord, which is in your lower back. Last but not least, the abdominal obliques draw in the sides of your waist and allow you to wear youthful clothes and retain a youthful figure.

THE YOGA OBLIQUE NERVE TONER

The position to assume (Figure 67)

1. Sit at the edge of the Yogi Bench, or of something equally low.
2. Your feet and knees comfortably relaxed and apart. (Heels about 14 inches apart.)
3. Drop your head between your knees, and
4. Hook your forearms under about the middle of your right thigh.

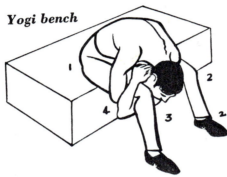

Yogi bench

Figure 67

How to do this simple movement (Figure 68)

5. Keep your forearms hooked under your right thigh, and
6. Straighten your knees by pulling your thigh-hooked forearms.
7. At the same time, twist your bent torso forwards to the right, so that your right shoulder is drawn downwards.
8. Your right-side abdominal muscles (your abdominal obliques) will contract hard the sides of your waist (*Figure 69*). Also *tremendous* for sides of thighs.

This simple movement physiologically:

1. Relieves popularity-decreasing neuralgia by stretching the nerves affected (*Figure 70*).
2. Draws in the sides of your waist, virtually like magic, enabling you to wear more youthful clothes. (*Figure 69*).

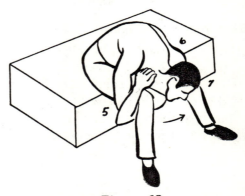

Figure 68

Figure 69

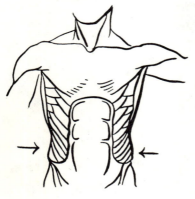

spine and
spinal cord

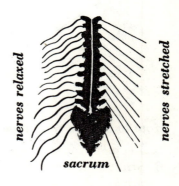

Figure 70

Frequency

5 times a day with *each* thigh, lowering left shoulder for left thigh.

Kavarzhan: the Yoga secret of the youthful, winning look—the look of popularity magic

Now that you have overcome the basic causes of the loss of your natural, inborn power of popularity, you are ready to crown it with the single most effective popularity multiplier of them all:

the carefully perfected, closely-guarded secret of the Kavarzhan. The Kavarzhan is the Yoga secret of the youthful look—and the youthful look *at any age* is popularity magic.

It is popularity magic because, first of all, it draws people to you much more easily. By wiping from ten to thirty (or even more) years of age from your face, Kavarzhan makes you look more like a youthful contemporary, rather than like someone from another era. Such a youthful look attracts far more people to you than before, for there are more younger people in the world than older folk. It fills you with confidence in yourself as an attraction, and that in itself refills you with the optimism, self-assurance and the assured manner that brings back to you in full your greatly reduced inborn popularity power: the power you started losing the moment the traumas of life started knocking it out of you.

The nucleus of the closely-guarded Yoga secret of Kavarzhan is the *parallel look*. For thousands of years the Yogis noticed that, as one grew older, noticeable wrinkles formed on his face, *not* so much from the natural process of aging, but principally from the skin-blows (skin-trauma) of daily use. And they observed that the skin-trauma was due to many causes, as follows:

1. The most important cause was the daily use of the mind in thinking, worrying, concentrating, emotional reactions, like anger, fear, watchfulness, hate, disappointment, envy and so on . . . use of the mind in striving for accuracy in occupation or in anything else, or in using the mind keenly for anything at all. Every serious use of the mind tensed all the muscles of the face, except the laughter muscles at the sides of the lips, and drew one's expression (just as it drew his vision) into a midline focus. His forehead, as a consequence, frowned vertically when he thought or meditated, or wrinkled horizontally when he was gripped with anxiety or fear. His eyes narrowed and formed crow's-feet when he stared closely or intently. His upper lip drew upwards in a sneer when he hated, and wrinkled under his nose; or it clamped shut when he was determined to overcome an obstacle, and hollowed his cheeks; or it pulled down at the corners of his mouth when he was depressed, discouraged, unhappy or ill and deepened the natural folds at their sides. Or his lower lip trembled and was drawn down tensely if he lived in constant tension and uncertainty, and wrinkled his chin.

2. One's geological environment added to these skin-traumas. Too much trauma from light in the eyes, as from direct sunshine outdoors, or from reflected sun off sand, water or snow, as well as the traumas of straining to see closely in poor light, plus the mechanical traumas of wind, dust and smoke, all caused him to frown and to narrow his eyes instinctively or consciously to protect them, thus wrinkling his forehead vertically and carving out crow's-feet beside his eyes.

3. Too much speaking pursed his lips excessively and lined them with wrinkles, like rays striking out from the sun.

4. Too much silence, on the other hand, atrophied his lip muscles and let his lips droop, and atrophied his cheek muscles, so that his cheeks hollowed and wrinkled deeply.

5. Too much smiling also carved out crow's-feet and deep, long wrinkles on the sides of his face, as well as deep wrinkles just under his chin.

6. Habitually walking or sitting with the head dropped more than it should be, carved out long, deep, parallel wrinkles on the neck and along its junction with the face.

7. Habitually walking or sitting with the head thrown back more than it should be, on the other hand, carved out wrinkles on the back of the neck at its junction with the back.

These different skin-blows (skin-traumas) did far more to form wrinkles on man's face than did the slow process of aging! But since man did think, and experienced emotion, and had to survive his environment, he could not escape skin-blows. The Yogi therefore created the secret Kavarzhan to nullify to a great extent the aging influences of these skin-blows on him, and did a tremendous job with it.

How to do Kavarzhan and regain the youthful, winning look— the look of popularity magic

The secret of Kavarzhan is the parallel look, followed by the facial gravity-angle surrender. Whenever you think, or resist, the skin-traumas of your environment, the muscles of your eyes and face contract and draw your eyes and the skin of your face inwards toward the midline, either vertically or horizontally, and even hold them in that position for a while after the traumas have passed, until your skin adopts that configuration permanently with wrinkles. The secret is to acquire the habit, or at least to do the simple routine, of preventing your eyes (and therefore the muscles of your face) from focusing inwards towards the midline, but of staying apart, instead, to their limit of full relaxation. So, follow the instructions closely.

A. How to Do the Parallel Look

Sit comfortably in a chair and gaze straight into the distance and think of nothing. Your eyes will relax and drift apart until they stare straight into space in parallel lines to each other. Your eyes are then in a state of rest, with their lens, their pupils and the muscles that bring them together in the midline, totally relaxed, for your eyes are then accommodated to their farthest point in vision. That's why it is relaxing to look far away. When all your eye muscles are relaxed, the muscles of your face follow suit reflexly. The muscles that wrinkle your forehead then relax; those that form crow's-feet beside your eyes relax; your sneering muscles relax; the tight lip muscles that bring on the antisocial look of angry old age, relax; the muscles that pull down the corners of your lips relax; and those that wrinkle your chin relax.

If you have access to no far away view, then look straight at two points on your wall, three inches apart. Let the space *between* the two points turn blurry to your sight and concentrate on seeing the left point with your left eye, and the right point with your right eye.

When you do the parallel look, your only face muscle that contracts is your laughing muscle. Follow the parallel look immediately with the facial gravity-angle surrender.

B. How to Do the Facial Gravity-Angle Surrender

When you sit or stand, gravity pulls downward the soft tissues of your face and erases, to a degree, the horizontal wrinkles on your forehead and your crow's-feet. When you lie down, gravity pulls outwards and downwards and erases, to a degree, your frown, the deep folds between your mouth and cheeks, your double chin if the pillow is low, the wrinkles around your ears, the sun-ray-like wrinkles lining your lips, and those at the corners of your mouth. That's why the relaxed corpse looks so much handsomer than the same man before he died.

But your mind *defies* these pulls of gravity on those muscles of your face and tenses them instead and wrinkles the skin of your face. You can overcome this defiance of your mind and smooth out the wrinkles on your face, beyond what the parallel look has already accomplished, with the facial gravity-angle surrender.

In order to smooth out the horizontal wrinkles on your forehead, your crow's-feet, your double chin and the wrinkles around your neck, maintain the parallel look, as soon as you do it, but drop your head back on your neck about 30 degrees. Keep your eyes fixed on the same spot in the far distance (or on the wall), and they will relax even more because you will no longer be holding them up to the horizontal level, but just letting them drop down as low as gravity will pull them. Let your jaw drop, too, with no resistance whatever to gravity. Like magic, your frowns and wrinkles flatten out to noticeable degrees. Maintain the position for ten seconds.

Close your eyes now and drop your head forwards gently towards your chest, and let your lower jaw hang towards the ground. Like magic, the wrinkles at the back of your neck, behind your ears, again those of your double chin and of the corners of your mouth, smooth out to noticeable degrees. Maintain the position for five seconds.

Do the whole procedure twice a day, or more if you wish. *That* is the Yoga secret of Kavarzhan. It has been altered only slightly from the original version. It is a miraculous facial rejuvenator.

Case histories

HOW LONESOME EDDIE QUICKLY REGAINED
ENOUGH NERVE-TONE TO BRING NEEDED ZEST
INTO HIS LONELY LIFE

Eddie was living for years in a big city, but was still lonesome, as is usually the case. Yet he knew there were people in it whom he'd like to know. In his own building he ran into some, occasionally, on the elevator. He opened conversations with some, but felt vaguely stiff and overcome with defeatism and failed to make anything of it. He wondered if he lacked the pep or whatever it took to push ahead in social life.

Eddie was in good health, but one side of his torso was notice-ably more developed than the other. I instantly realized that, even though it did not show up on X-ray, he was suffering from reduced all-over Spino-Volt and hence, of reduced nerve-tone.

I taught him the Yoga oblique nerve-tone. He felt stiff at first because he had never "stretched" his spine so fully, he said. Soon after doing it, though, he was flooded with an ebullient energy which he never remembered enjoying before. "Feel like I'm walking on air!" he exclaimed.

After doing it regularly for less than a fortnight, he started facing people he'd like to meet with an attitude that drew them to him in seemingly irresistible fashion, and it filled him with such overwhelming confidence in himself that he found himself saying the right things to them automatically and attracting them to him. Within another fortnight he had attracted enough new friends to him to start enjoying a delightful social life. With Yoga for popularity, backward, lonesome Eddie had quickly regained enough of his natural, inborn nerve-tone to enable him to step right out and attract to him, in a surprisingly short time, a delightful group of people into an informal group and bring needed zest into his lonely life.

How 49-Year-Old Whining Alfred, Who Was Avoided Generally, Swept People Off Their Feet by Relieving His Subchronic Aches and Pains

Alfred, 49 years old, was universally called a tiresome pest, a "wet blanket," a "drip," and other such epithets. "No matter how happy everybody is before *he* comes around," people would say, "the moment he steps in, all the fun goes out!" People sighed in despair when they couldn't avoid meeting him. Alfred hadn't the least idea what was wrong either, except that he felt humili-atingly cold-shouldered by everybody. He changed his manner time and again to see if it made any difference, but it did not.

Alfred grew interested in Yoga because he wanted to reduce his waist. He thought, for some reason or other, that his shapeless waist was causing his unpopularity.

He stripped, and I saw the tight muscles on his lower back. Since he was far from being an athlete, I questioned him and found out that he detested damp weather because he felt it at once in his back. Then he let loose a tirade against the weather, politicians, demonstrations, stock market manipulators, cheating wives, fixed fights, "ambulance chasers," and so forth. He had a sour attitude towards everything.

I was not posing as a psychiatrist, but Alfred seemed to be normal enough mentally otherwise and had a perfect work and domestic life record. I asked him more about his lower back, and he confessed that, upon exposure to dampness, he experienced vague pains and tenderness around his kidneys which lasted for weeks. All during that time he felt a bit inadequate, as if something wasn't quite right with him, and it made him angry at the world.

I concluded that the irritations of the condition had impressed themselves into his mind repeatedly and soured his whole attitude. I showed him how to loosen and keep limber the tight muscles in his lower back.

In three days Alfred felt like a different person already, and his caustic attitude towards everything sweetened noticeably. His conversation altered, and he grew more witty and philosophical. To his amazement he was attracting people to him now as he had not done in a long time. By the end of the week he loosened his tight lower back muscles practically to normal and released his natural, inborn charm and wit.

How Grouchy, Friendless Jimmy, Who Looked Like 65 at 55, Regained a Youthful Look to His Face

Grouchy, ignored, friendless Jimmy looked 65 at 55 and was so completely out of everything that he was tempted to take his own life. He tried to make friends, but he couldn't draw people to him. Yet, he was generous and kindhearted and would do anything for anyone who showed him the least appreciation. He was only 55, too; so he didn't see why he should be out of everything. Still, he felt like a social misfit, as if he no longer belonged on this planet. Jimmy had never been a good mixer, but now he was actually *avoided* by people when he tried to join a lively, interesting group, and he was acutely sensitive to the cold-shoulder treatment he received. And so he became grouchy, and that left him still more friendless and ignored.

Jimmy confided his troubles to me. His expression was grave

and serious, making him look older, too. When he sought the company of people ten years or so younger than he, he said, he expected them to accept him as practically a contemporary of theirs. Instead, they viewed him as a *senior citizen!* "I'll be a senior citizen fast enough some day!" he raged to me. "In the meantime, though, I'd like to pass for at least ten years younger than I am!"

It was obvious that Jimmy's deep-seated wish to look and be considered significantly younger than he was, had played havoc with his personality. So, I did nothing more than show him how to do Kavarzhan. Within a month Jimmy seemed to look so much younger and amiable that he was already making friends with a speed he had never expected. People who saw him six months later, said to me that he appeared to be 15 to 20 years younger, and that his taut, habitual expression had altered into a pleasant, endearing one that made him instantly sought-after wherever he went. With Kavarzhan, grouchy, ignored, friendless Jimmy, who looked like 65 at 55, had regained a youthful look to his face which brought it a pleasant, endearing aspect that made him popular with everyone.

Summary of the steps for using secrets for popularity

In order to apply the Yoga secrets for popularity, you have to counteract the physical distortions and their undermining effects on your body caused by the four horsemen of the mastabah. You do so by:

1. Loosening and keeping limber the tight muscles that bring on subchronic lumbago, subchronic rheumatism, uneven muscular development, or other related subchronic conditions in you which cause muscle strain.
2. Counteracting the structural distortions on you of abnormal positions maintained regularly from bad habit or from your occupation.
3. Relieving the devitalizing subchronic aches and pains arising from subclinical (unfelt) squeezing of your spinal nerves.
4. Increasing your nerve-tone.
5. Regaining the youthful, winning look—the look of popularity magic—with Kavarzhan.

Yoga Secrets for Leadership

12

Since the Yogis practically withdraw from the active world and live solitary lives, it is difficult to conceive of them developing an incredible power of leadership. Adepts, though, do seek them out, and every Yogi enjoys having at least two or three of them settled in his general vicinity, at his beck and call. To achieve that goal is nothing short of miraculous when you realize that the Yogi offers the adept very little in return. In most instances the Yogi does not even bother to teach the adept anything, but just advises him to find his own cave and start meditating day and night for the next ten years or more, until he either gives up in despair or develops into a Yogi himself. The Yogi holds out no utopian reward to him for his great sacrifices either, but only a lonely, poverty-stricken, materially-deprived life in the wilderness or at the fringe of the Indian desert.

The Yogi, it is obvious, must certainly possess a power of leadership which is practically impossible to equal, much less surpass. And it is not an accidental power that he happened to discover, but one which he has perfected because he *needs and wants* adepts near him, for he is still a human being. In his later years, too, he yearns to pass on some of his lifetime of accumulated knowledge to another. Since he has to compete with other Yogis in his vicinity for adepts, besides, he keeps his secrets of

156

leadership well guarded. The secrets of those with many "enslaved" adepts have now been carefully studied and refined for *your own use* in the Western world, to enable you to gain the utmost benefit from them as quickly as possible, without subjecting yourself to their wearying disciplines. The case histories following these secrets prove how effective they can be for you.

The four horsemen reduce your natural, inborn power of leadership by:

1. Shortening your back more than normally; decreasing your height; flattening your chest, and bulging out your abdominal hollow.
2. Weakening your calves and your feet.

You will now be shown how the four horsemen bring on those unwanted changes in you and reduce your natural, inborn power of leadership, and the refined, scientifically perfected Yoga secrets for counteracting them and acquiring leadership over others swiftly.

How the four horsemen reduce your natural, inborn power of leadership

In order to lead others most easily and successfully, you have to *look like a leader*. You have to present yourself at your full height, with your chest up, and your abdomen flat. When your back slumps and shortens your height, and your chest slumps and bulges your belly, you look more like a comedian or a faithful follower than like a leader. First impressions are most important for leadership, and you present your best first impression when you stand at your full height, hold your head straight, keep your chest up, and your belly in. You must *assume* that posture and *maintain* it against the relentless battering of these four horsemen. Good posture, besides, is not enough, unless you first re-elongate your spine back to its normal length at your age, so that you can stand or sit at full normal height. Not only do you display yourself at your best physical proportions then, but also you are at your tallest and even appear *several inches taller* than you measure. Your vertebral openings, too, are opened at their widest, and your Spino-Volt can be fired through your spinal nerve at its strongest and supercharge you with the utmost drive for leadership.

You already know that you are taller after a good long sleep than you are at bedtime, by as much as one-half to three-fourths of an inch, or more. By bedtime your segmented spine has sagged, and your spinal disks have shrunken. All your vertebral openings, as a result, are narrowed still more than they are structurally, and squeeze your spinal nerves still harder. Your blood vessels are therefore conveying less blood to your muscles and organs than they did in the morning, and your muscles are responding more slowly and less powerfully to your brain commands, because your Spino-Volt has been correspondingly reduced.

All day long, though, this condition has been gradually occurring, and the Spino-Volt to your most vitally essential organs, such as your heart, liver, stomach, lungs, brain, kidney and glands, is being lessened. Since these most vitally essential organs can't grow once you are an adult, as your muscles do through use, and make up for their decreased functional capacity, they cannot make up for the lessened Spino-Volt they receive. Your whole body suffers, for that reason, and you don't feel as strong at bedtime as when you arise. Your natural, inborn power of leadership is, therefore, being reduced all day long and leaving you more crabby and argumentative instead. To be a real leader, then, you have to present yourself at your full height, with your chest up and your abdominal hollow evident, so that your vertebral openings will be kept wider opened and not decrease unnecessarily your natural, inborn Spino-Volt.

How to "grow taller," and regain lost, natural, inborn power of leadership at any age

Unless you are doing them under doctor's orders, *avoid* exercises that bend your spine backwards. Those who do them risk wearing down the backs of their spinal disks and bringing the tail ends of their vertebrae nearer towards each other. If the exercises are done for years, the tail ends of such vertebrae may eventually touch and *lock*, causing a vertebral fixation. Many a back-bending acrobat, and many unscientific practitioners of Yoga, have suffered that fate. So, just do the following simple Yogatone movements for "growing" taller, raising your chest and decreasing your abodminal bulge. (*Figures 71–73*).

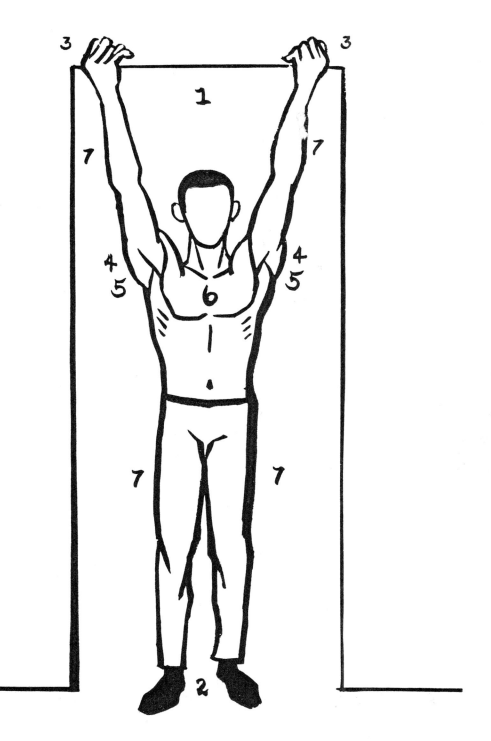

Figure 71

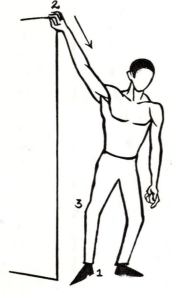

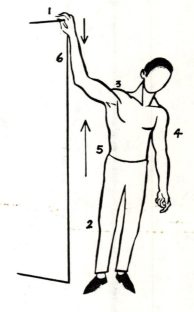

Figure 72   *Figure 73*

THE TWO-ARM DOORWAY PULL

The position to assume (Figure 71).

1. Stand beside a doorway with a strong top, or beside an opened door.
2. Feet hip-width apart. (About 8 inches).
3. Grasp close to the ends of the door or doorway. (If you are too short, stand on a box, a pile of old magazines or anything stable and high enough.) Grasp with fingers only. If the door edges are sharp, wear cheap cloth gloves.

How to do this simple movement (Figure 71).

4. Pull downwards hard with your shoulders.
5. Contract hard your upper, outer back muscles as you do so.
6. Inhale as you pull downwards.
7. Keep arms, knees and body straight.
8. Hold for two seconds. Then relax.

This simple movement develops:

1. Upper section of latissimus dorsi (*Figure 71–3*).
2. Under sides of forearms.
3. Broadens shoulders enormously.
4. Strengthens hands and wrists.
5. Straightens back, and therefore increases your height back to what it should be.
6. Raises chest.

Frequency

2–5 repetitions a day. This simple movement is truly simple but brings surprising results.

THE ONE-ARM DOORWAY PULL

The position to assume (Figure 72).

1. Stand beside an opened door, with feet hip-width (about 8 inches) apart.
2. Grasp the corner of the door with your left hand. (Put a pad under the hand.)
3. If you are tall, bend your knees in order to straighten the arm stiffly. If you are short, stand on a secure box or stool, if necessary.

How to do this simple movement (Figure 73).

1. Pull down hard with the left hand, until
2. It straightens your knees,
3. Lifts your left shoulder up high, and
4. Bends your body at the waist, over to the right.

This simple movement develops:

1. Upper half of the latissimus dorsi. It is very effective and easy to do (*Figure 73—5*).
2. Wears off fat from the sides of the body, for it stretches them.
3. Stretches the myotomic muscles of the vertebrae, and so allows the spine to lengthen out more and increase the height.
4. Also contracts the myotomic muscles of the vertebrae, on

the opposite side of those that stretch, thereby strengthening your spine.

5. Abdominal oblique muscles (of the contracting, shortened
   side).
6. Under side of forearm of holding hand (*Figure 73–6*).

Frequency

2–5 repetitions a day, with *each* hand.

•To keep strain off the door hinges, place a small wedge under the bottom
of the free end of the door (*Figure 73–7*).

Myo-tensing: the Yoga secret for influencing others

Myo-tensing is considered by the Yogis to be the most effective
tool for bringing others swiftly under your control, and with the
greatest of ease—even if you are as much as 40 feet away from
them—just so long as they can perceive you distinctly. Furthermore, you do myo-tensing invisibly, unsuspectedly (beneath your
clothes).

Its secret is based on the fact that much of what is ponderously
explained as the effect of mind over the whole body, is made
simple and easily understood when it is realized that it is *not* the
mind, but the little nerve segments of the brain which affect
bodily activities. Strength comes, in other words, not because of
the *consciousness* of strength, but the consciousness of strength
comes because the little nerve segments of the brain are stimulated in a certain manner. By contracting a certain muscle or
group of muscles, in brief, you stimulate certain little nerve segments of your brain, and that brings you the consciousness of
strength.

You don't have to develop huge strength in the larger muscles
of your body in order to acquire that feeling, either. On the contrary, you just have to contract those larger muscles secretly and
invisibly whenever you desire to fill your mind with the consciousness of strength, and hold the contraction *no longer than
two seconds*. The contraction will flash immediately a steady
stream of *power-sensations* to the little nerve segments of your
brain, and you will be filled with a confidence, optimism and a
feeling of invincibility which converts you at once into a leader.
That is the scientific basis of the Yoga secret of myo-tensing.

Myo·tensing: how to influence and control a person with the Latpector

With simple, invisible, unsuspected myo·tensing you can grip anyone you wish with your mere presence, and influence him and attain your goals in life much more easily. If you are small in stature or position, and face a bigger man, you can bring him down to a size and position *smaller than you*, psychologically speaking, with a brief contraction of a secret muscle-combine. That man will be taken aback by the inexplicable fearlessness of his size or authority which he suddenly senses in you, and he will lose confidence in himself and let *you* control *him*, instead of *him* controlling *you*. (This technique is commonly used in all therapies, when a healthy part is stimulated to heal the sick part reflexly. The little boy, too, feels as strong as the big boy when he flexes his little biceps hard. Furthermore, it can even be applied over the telephone.) The most well-guarded Yoga myo· tensing secret for influencing and controlling anybody you wish invisibly, when you are *sitting*, is the Latpector. You will be taught that one first.

How to Do the Latpector

The Latpector is the most well-guarded of all the myo·tensing Yoga secrets because it is not only the easiest one to do, but also it is the most effective one, by far, for influencing and controlling anybody you wish instantly, invisibly and unsuspectedly, particularly when you are sitting. It was extremely difficult to attain this Yoga secret. It works so effectively because it fills your body instantly with a sensation of possessing a gigantic torso, both chesty and broad-backed, no matter how flat-chested or narrow-shouldered you might actually be. And that sensation, reflexly, flashes to your conscious mind a tremendous Spino-Volt of invincible psychological power which the other person senses by your manner, and it stuns him and subjects him to you. So, master this easy, but nothing less than magical, muscle-combine contraction for instant use anywhere, any time, and with anybody, as follows.

Suppose you are suddenly confronted with an ominous situation —one for which you had no time to prepare beforehand, but which requires an immediate defense, explanation, or countering action on your part. The situation may involve your social life, your business life, your romantic life, or even your personal safety. To delay prompt action could compromise you or leave you open to disaster. So tightly are you gripped with fear because of it that you can hardly think of what to say or do.

There is *one thing* you *have to do* at once, before all is lost. You have to banish *all fear* instantly from you. *Then* you can think clearly and meet the situation squarely.

Banish all fear instantly from you by Yoga Macro-Muscle-Toning your back, chest and triceps muscles combined. This is how you do it—stand perfectly still and face the ominous situation, with your arms hanging limply at your sides. Now, draw your shoulders slightly *backwards and downwards*, and then *inwards*, hard. Your triceps, your outer back muscles and your chest muscles, will contract vigorously, as if trying to squeeze your body into your spine. Maintain the contraction for two seconds. Then relax.

Blood will flush these muscles and give you a chesty, broad-back feeling. This feeling will flash into your conscious mind and influence it with the sensation that you are much bigger and broader-shouldered than you actually are. Since you cannot see your chest or back at the time, *your mind* accepts that picture as *fact*, and fills you with the confidence that you *are* much bigger, and stronger, than you actually are. Your fears are routed at once, because you now envision yourself as a *far more capable* person than when you were frozen with fear. Hence, you think clearly, meet the ominous situation squarely, and conquer it.

Benefits of the Latpector

Practice the Latpector with the woman you want to impress, "facing" you in the mirror, and it will fill you with the confidence to sweep her off her feet with your manliness. Practice it imagining yourself taking an oral examination before a panel of examiners, and you will fill yourself with the calm and assurance to pass it successfully. Practice it by imagining yourself taking a written examination, and it will fill you with the confidence of passing it easily, so that your mind will function as it never has before, aided remarkably by your set-free subconscious mind. Even practice it pretending to talk to someone over the telephone. The Yogis made a historic, and yet incredibly simple, discovery when they came upon the secret of the Latpector for gigantic psychological achievement. No wonder they have guarded it so carefully!

How to myo-tense and attain psychologic leadership over others when standing

Your front thigh muscles are the muscles which the Yogis found were the most effective for filling the conscious mind with the most power to influence and control anybody you wish, with a secret, simple, invisible muscle contraction when *standing*. Contracting *no other* muscle group in your body equals it for filling you so fully with self-confidence, optimism and invincibility when standing. The reasons are too numerous to mention, but probably the most important is that your front thigh muscles are exceptionally long and thick. Hence, they straighten your torso, overcome the downpull of gravity on your erect posture, and endow you with a sensation of being light, young, elegant and quick-witted. Myo-tensing your front thigh muscles, besides, squeezes the veins of your thighs and quickens the return of the blood from your legs to your lungs and heart; and therefore, to your brain, thereby reducing your sense of fatigue and increasing your feeling of elation. A rush of nerve electricity then floods your conscious mind and restores you your lost, natural, inborn power of leadership. So, master this simple, effortless, invisible, but magic, use of a group of muscles, as discovered and kept closely-guarded by the Yogis.

How to Myo-Tense Your Front Thigh Muscles

1. Stand to one side of your mirror; then stroll up and stand before it with a mild expression.
2. Let your heels stand about six inches apart, with your toes pointed outwards about 30 degrees to keep you balanced without strain.
3. Now, lock (straighten) your knees, and tense the fronts of your thighs hard. The harder the better.
4. Hold the contraction for two seconds.
5. Then relax.

The muscles of the front of your thighs will throb, as if swelling fast. And the moment you relax, a sensation of warm blood rushing into them will seize you. Your thighs will feel firm, young and springy, like those of a male ballet dancer.

That is how to myo-tense your front thigh muscles. It could be no more simple. Practice it before your mirror about three or four times.

Rest or do nothing else for at least five minutes, and then repeat it. This time, though, visualize yourself doing it before an *audience*. It will fill you with a confidence and optimism in your ability to lead everyone that will virtually enslave them to you before you utter a word.

Myo-tense your front thigh muscles several times, unsuspectedly, invisibly, during the course of your speech to the audience, and you will retain that invincible attitude in you until the end of it. It will also banish fatigue from you by repeatedly toning up your anti-gravity muscles and easing the load off your heart.

Case histories

How Sidney Toned Up His Latpector Muscles for Confidence to Land the Big Position He Wanted

Sidney was a small, nervous man. He was dissatisfied with his job because he was getting nowhere in it and because it offered him little opportunity for advancement. He was no longer young either, and his children were nearing college age. Sidney felt increasingly miserable because so many other men he knew were advancing amazingly, and yet he was convinced that he had more to offer than they. But he lacked the courage and confidence to go out and try for something that might give him the chance to use his talents. He always took the back seat and let others who didn't compare with him take the wheel. He was never the leader, but always the follower. True, he was somewhat short and puny, but the world abounded with short, puny men who had been great leaders.

He also lacked the amount of college education so many others had.

Sidney confided his problem to me. I noticed that he had allowed his spine to "shorten," and that his posture, in general, was that of someone who had not exercised systematically for some time, and who was therefore flabby from head to foot. Even his walk demonstrated that.

I taught him, first of all, how to re-elongate his spine with Yogatone. And then I taught him how to myo-tense both the Latpector and his front thigh muscles.

The next time I saw Sidney he already looked taller, was holding his head higher and was getting eager to apply for a promising position he saw advertised. I thought it was too soon for him to try, but the psychological impact of these swift (even if still inconsiderable) changes in him had already awakened his natural, inborn confidence and optimism for leadership so strongly that I did not bother to dissuade him.

So, Sidney went ahead. His prospective employer turned out to be a huge man who dwarfed Sidney, both in height and in shoulder width. Sidney's knees quaked as he confronted him in the office for the interview, and he could already see his dreams collapsing again. The huge man took one look at him and started to hem and haw and glance at his watch. "It's now or never," Sidney mumbled to himself and sank lifelessly into the chair indicated to him by the enormous but unwelcoming hand. His heart was savagely battering down his chest, and Sidney felt like leaping to his feet and fleeing.

Instead, he at once did the Latpector invisibly, unsuspectedly, beneath his clothes. In an instant his chest felt big and bulging (even though it was far from being so), and his back felt thick and broad. But since Sidney could not see how small and insignificant they still were, but could only *feel* how big and powerful they suddenly seemed to be, the mental reproduction of their sudden giant-size and power flashed into his mind. Immediately, he felt that he could thrash that mammoth of a man any time, or outclass him in business or romance.

Sidney landed the much-coveted position. The Latpector muscle-combine, two-second contraction had filled Sidney with enough confidence and feeling of invincibility to assume the leadership over the giant, important employer before him and to win him the big position he wanted.

How Elford, Suddenly Promoted to a Position of
Leadership in His Company, Saved Himself from Being
Ousted from It Because of His Inability to Lead

Elford had waited for years for the very promotion he dreamed
about. He had missed it repeatedly, but this time he had climbed
into it. He only had to be successful in it, and a vice-presidency
would be assured him.

Once in his new position, though, Elford discovered that he
lacked the talent to lead subordinates! He was not a "born"
leader!

Gripped with terror, he revealed his problem to me. I was not
surprised, because Elford dragged himself around with his chest
sunken, his abdomen bulging, and without spring in his step, as
if his leg and foot muscles were made of putty. Upon observing
him standing and moving, hardly a subordinate would view him
as a leader. They would show it in their demeanor and rip the
confidence out of Elford. It was impossible for Elford to lead
subordinates with any facility while he remained like that.

I taught Elford how to "grow taller," raise his chest, increase
his abdominal hollow, tone up his calves and myo-tense the fronts
of his thighs. Within two weeks he had his problem far better
under control. He stood now more like someone of importance;
he moved with a suggestion of a spring in his step; and when he
stood and dealt with his subordinates, he myo-tensed the fronts
of his thighs and they felt pillar-like to him, as if he were the
Rock of the company. With the resulting psychological impact,
he *acted* like the Rock of the company, and his subordinates
started accepting him as if he *were*. Two months later, he was
called in, praised, and practically promised a vice-presidency
within a year. Elford had saved himself from being ousted from
his new position for lacking the ability to lead, by toning up his
calves and myo-tensing the muscles of the fronts of his thighs.

Summary of the steps using Yoga secrets for leadership

In order to apply the Yoga secrets for leadership, you have to
counteract the physical detriments and their effects on yourself
and others caused by the four horsemen of the mastabah. You
do so by:

1. Growing "taller," raising your chest and decreasing your abdominal bulge.
2. Myo·tensing secret groups of muscles.
3. Toning up your foot and calf muscles and adding a youthful spring to your step.

The dragging mental and physical influences on you which reduce your natural, inborn power of leadership will be lifted from you, and you will tear yourself free from the shackles that bind you, and burst forth as an unconquerable person who leads others with comparative ease.

Yoga
Secrets for
the
Executive   13
and
Professional
Man

Since Yogis do not run businesses or enter professional careers, it is difficult to understand, at first, what they could offer for maximum success in such careers. But the Yogi *does* have a career. He is the world's greatest rugged individualist, and he picks his own career and sets out to climb the heights in it, no matter how rough the road. He just does not seek material rewards for his efforts. But he does have a career!

Indeed, there is no tougher, or more time-consuming, career to pursue! It demands the deepest concentration, the most tireless patience, the greatest determination, the soundest health and strength, the keenest originality, the utmost confidence and optimism, the most absolute freedom from pain or fatigue, the strongest resistance against boredom, the best long-maintained posture, the longest healthy life possible, the fewest vacations imaginable, and possesses the least certainty of success.

No prospective executive or professional man in the western world would even consider such a career, not only because of its doubtful material rewards, but also because of its excessive rigors. But since the Yogi does select and pursue it to the end, he has to prepare his mind and body to carry through his efforts successfully. For that reason, he has mastered secrets of success which outclass those of any in the Western world. These well-guarded

Yoga secrets have now been carefully studied and scientifically refined for *your own use*, to enable you to gain the utmost benefit from them as quickly as possible, without subjecting yourself to their wearying disciplines.

How the four horsemen of the mastabah reduce your natural, inborn powers to succeed as an executive or professional man

The four horsemen reduce your natural inborn powers to succeed at your best as an executive or professional man by:

1. Softening the deep muscles of your spine (your myotomic muscles) and thereby "crippling" it.
2. Plaguing you with middle back pain.
3. "Crippling" your neck.
4. Constipating you.

You will now be shown how the four horsemen bring on these unwanted changes in you and reduce your natural, inborn powers to succeed at your best as an excutive or professional man, and the refined, scientifically-perfected Yoga secrets for counteracting them and achieving swiftly the utmost benefits from them for your career.

How the four horsemen soften the deep muscles of your back (your myotomic muscles) and thereby "cripple" it

The deep (myotomic) muscles of your back are those that straighten it and keep it in the best balanced anti-gravity posture all day long, as you go about your daily life. They extend from the base of your spine to the base of your skull.

Your myotomic muscles vary in size to quite a degree, and act chiefly on your spine. The shorter ones extend between two adjoining vertebrae and straighten those two alone. The longer ones extend over several vertebrae and either straighten all of them, or just straighten the first and last ones of that group. In that way, your myotomic muscles control the individual movements of each, or several, of your vertebrae, and keep your giant, flexible, jointed spinal column always ready to adjust itself, day and night, to your thousands of body movements. When toned up, your myotomic muscles do an efficient job and keep your individual vertebrae lined up with each other, with their vertebral openings as wide as possible to allow the greatest Spino-Volt power to flow through the spinal nerves.

Over the years, though, as a result of the long hours of sitting or standing every day in your office; of social life, driving, and lack of scientific exercise, the deep muscles of your back lose considerable power to keep your vertebrae properly in line with each other, or to draw them back into line as you go about your daily chores.

Your back, as a consequence, acquires wrong-back curves and you settle into faulty posture. The muscles of your lower back then tighten to balance your imbalanced back against the down-pull of gravity and bring on insidious and nagging (even if sub-chronic) backache which continually harrasses you and increases the supersensitivity of the pain-carrying nerves of that area. Your conscious mind, as a result, becomes accustomed to receiving pain from it and comes to *expect and look forward* to that pain. The vertebral openings of the resulting wrong-back curves are narrowed still more and squeeze still more the spinal nerves passing through them, and reduce the potency of their Spino-Volts. And so, your back habitually feels tight in different places, and throbs with hot and cold sensations that are difficult to pinpoint. Even when you lie down and try to rest, it throbs. You wish that some-one would pound it with a sledgehammer and smash the misery out of it. Your humor has left you, and a frown has deepened your brow. Your lips turn down more than up, and your head is held less straight. Problems in your work which were comparatively easy to meet before, seem unconquerable now because you lose your patience soon and give up. Your best judgment has dis-appeared, robbing you of confidence and filling you with dread. That heightens the activity of your sympathetics (your fighting nerves) and increases your body acidity, ill-humor, ill-temper and nervous tension. And that is only the beginning of the long line of increasingly crippling symptoms which will assail you.

How to tone up your flabby myotomic muscles with Yogatone and rid yourself of damaging ill-temper and nervous tension

The increasingly painful symptoms and effects of the four horsemen on you can be banished by toning up your myotomic muscles once every day with a few simple, scientifically-refined,

Yoga movements. These are The Wing Swing and The Upwards Eagle Spread which are described as follows:

THE WING SWING

The position to assume

1. Sit on a chair, or stand. It might be easier to do this simple movement at first standing up, and learn quickly how to do it right.
2. Hold arms out at sides, elbows down, palms down, but palms (relaxed) held higher than the elbows.

How to do this simple movement

3. Swing arms around in a circle. Swing them first backwards and upwards, then downwards and forwards. The contractions of the muscles being used, occur on the backwards and upwards parts of the swing. These muscles relax when your arms swing forwards and downwards. Actually, you swing your *shoulders*, and your arms swing with them.
4. Inhale as your shoulders swing backwards and upwards.
5. Exhale as they swing forwards and downwards. Do the simple movement vigorously, fast, but completely, making complete circles with your shoulders.

This simple movement tones up:

1. The myotomic muscles of your upper back. It also develops
2. The muscles that cap your shoulders and make them look broader (when your arms and shoulders swing upwards).
3. The muscles at the back of your shoulders, when your arms and shoulders swing backwards.

Frequency

5 repetitions a day. Swing and rotate your shoulders around like a big bird about to take to flight. This is an exhilarating, simple movement.

THE UPWARDS EAGLE SPREAD

The position to assume

1. Stand with feet hip-width (8 inches apart).

2. Hold a rolled magazine or newspaper in back of you.
3. Hands close together.
4. Palms facing backwards.
5. Back straight.
6. Draw shoulders high up.
7. Exhale and expand your chest.

How to do this simple movement

1. Exhale,
2. Arch your back, and
3. Draw hands backwards and upwards *as far as you can*, tightening your upper middle back muscles into powerful knots. Keep shoulders DRAWN UP.
4. Hold for two seconds. Then relax.

This simple movement tones up and develops:

1. The myotomic muscles of the upper half of your back. Also develops your
2. Trapezius.
3. Levator scapulae. (Without this muscle developed, you have a narrow, weak-looking neck.)
4. Posterior deltoid.
5. Triceps (inner).
6. Forearms (underside).

Frequency

2–5 times a day; 3 times a week.

Important: This simple movement will change the whole contour of your upper back.

Expand your chest and arch your back a little when you do the simple movement. *Even more effective* when done with *palms forwards*.

Results

With your myotomic muscles toned up, your whole body and mind undergo a great change for the better. Your myotomic muscles will then pull more evenly on both sides of your spine, bring your vertebrae back into line as much as possible and smooth out your wrong-back curves in the same proportion. No longer overstrained by the four horsemen, your myotomic muscles lose their fatigue and can combat the continuing pounding of the "four enemies" more easily. No longer does your back habitually feel tired or tight in different places, with hot and cold sensations throbbing here and there mysteriously. Your good humor returns, and the gloomy frown deserts your brow. Your lips arch back up, and you hold your head straight again. Problems in your life again grow easier to solve, and your patience and determination return. You can think deeply once more, use your best judgment, and regain your lost confidence. Your ill-temper and nervous tension disappear as if by magic.

How your habitual faulty posture curses you with middle back pain

As an executive or professional man, you are not subject as much to the traumas of weight-bearing, as to those of a bent back while you sit daily in your office, for hours at a time. The invariable result is middle back pain. It strikes you between your shoulder blades and feels as if you've been stabbed in the back. It is considered a minor condition, but it *does not feel minor to you.* Few minor conditions affecting human beings can be more distressing. (It may also be directly brought on by a draft of cold air, dampness, infection, a spinal disk lesion, a tumor, or some other cause requiring a physician's care; so, always have it checked.) The aggravating pain occurs at various times and stiffens and limits your shoulder movements. Your shoulders, indeed, feel as if strapped in a strait-jacket, for your least attempt to move them brings you grief. Because of this, even if the pain is subchronic, you instinctively try to move your shoulders as little as possible, and that causes their muscles to atrophy and your shoulders themselves to hunch and narrow. You even find it difficult to stand and walk straight, and so you appear shorter, narrow shouldered and round-backed, and therefore, older. You might even feel pain (even if subchronic) at the back of your neck.

Thirty per cent of all individuals in the middle-age group who presented shoulder complaints, either from traumas or not, were found to have the middle back pain (scapulocostal) syndrome. All these symptoms are far less acute—indeed, they are likely to remain subchronic—when due solely to your faulty posture in your office, driving your car, carrying parcels, and so forth. But the nagging ache and pain, and the degree of stiffness and tenderness in your middle back build up, in the course of time, an area of tension and tenderness between your shoulder blades which alternates with a throbbing numbness that makes sitting at your desk a gruesome ordeal and seriously diminishes your attention to your work. The vicious circle proceeds until you subconsciously deplore your occupation and yearn to flee from it altogether.

Long before it reaches that stage (that is, while it is still in the subchronic stage and is still manifesting itself occasionally only with burdensome nagging aches and pains), it is already flashing messages of subclinical pain to your *subconscious mind* and already turning you against your work, although you don't suspect why. It is time to start counteracting it at once. Middle back pain is one of the worst ailments that threaten the Yogi, for he sits for very long periods of time, practically every day, in his rigorous disciplines and long meditations. He has therefore perfected a way to overcome it while it is still in the subchronic stage, so that he can always feel ready to carry on his perfectioning every day. The Ergo-Cross is the scientific refinement of his simple Yogatone movement to achieve that goal.

The ergo-cross: for toning up the necessary muscles to overcome subchronic middle back pain

THE ERGO-CROSS

How to do this simple movement

1. Sit in a chair, with arms hanging loosely at the sides.
2. Palms inwards (or facing each other).
3. Raise arms up to shoulder level, and as far back as possible.
4. Your back will hunch.
5. Hold for two seconds. Then relax.

This simple movement tones up:

1. Upper portions of trapezius.
2. Rhomboids.

Tense these muscles as hard as you can.

Frequency

1–2 times a day. More if middle back pain is persistent.

Result

The stagnant blood pools which have accumulated in the soft tissues between your shoulder blades are squeezed out into your general circulation by your contracting and relaxing your trapezius muscles in the ergo-cross. That dissipates the tension they brought to bear on the endings of your pain-carrying nerves. Once more your shoulders feel free to move in any direction without being halted by pain (even if subchronic), and you can again square them, look broader, walk straight, show your natural height, and suggest more youth. Again you love your work and are eager to further your success in it. You become so enthusiastic again, in fact, that you can hardly quit your office at the end of the day.

Daily, while at your desk, or driving your car, walking, eating, or participating in social life, you hold your neck for many hours at a time either in an unnatural swan-like curve, or in a forward drop. That position stretches unduly the muscles at the sides and front of your neck, while it contracts excessively the muscles at the back, and those at the base of your skull. Your back is held in a humped position, in other words, and your neck curves, on top of it, with a swan-like, backward bend which narrows considerably, during those hours, all the vertebral openings in your spine between the base of your skull, down to about four inches below the base of your neck. This faulty posture creates a pressure about your neck similar to that of arthritis of the neck, so that the spinal nerves which pass through its considerably narrowed vertebral openings to supply the muscles of your scalp, neck, shoulders, arms and chest, are squeezed extraordinarily for hours every day, plaguing you with subchronic headache, neuritis and weakness. As a result, the blood circulation to your brain is disturbed, and your heart does not accelerate when called upon by your body to do so. All of this crushes your optimism and routs your calm thinking, and you become disgruntled and wish for an absolute change in everything. The Yogis, due to their rigorous disciplines in one seated position for hours at a time, are forced constantly to combat this condition and prevent it from turning acute. They do it with the Sitting Duck posture as follows:

THE SITTING DUCK

The position to assume

1. Sit comfortably in a chair.
2. Fold your hands, palms facing forwards, against your forehead. (Or hold a rolled newspaper or magazine across your forehead.)
3. Sit straight, but
4. Draw your neck backwards "militarily" straight.

How to do this simple movement

5. Resist hard with your folded hands, and
6. Force your head forwards.
7. Repeat.

This simple movement develops:

1. The sterno-mastoid muscles of both sides of your neck. It fills up impressively the base of your neck, making your neck look much shorter and thicker. Removes from your neck that weak-looking, fowl-neck look. And if your neck is fat and too bulky looking, it will wear the fat off and give it a strong, young look.

Frequency

8–10 repetitions; 3 times a week.

How your daily occupation saddles you with constipation

Sitting at your desk, in your car and other places all day long, or even just standing or moving about within a limited area, cannot help but saddle you with constipation, mild or severe. Even if your bowels move regularly, you may still be constipated because a certain amount of fecal matter may be regularly retained in your lower bowel and gradually deposited on its sides. (That is the leading cause of bulging diverticuli.) You are also threatened by hemorrhoids. Long before those pathological conditions come about, though, you will suffer from enragingly annoying discomforts which impair the joy in your work and reduce your normal efficiency.

As the hours pass at work, invisible, relentless gravity seizes you around the shoulders and presses your body down harder and harder on your seat, flattening out the big muscles and fat of your buttocks against it. Millions of capillaries in your buttocks are broken, and the area turns numb from the resulting blood congestion set up in it. Reflexly, through your interconnecting spinal nerves, the condition spreads to your rectum and your adjoining lower bowel, and the fecal matter there dries up abnormally and forms a short, hard mass. When you try to move your bowels the next day, this short, hard mass remains immovable, like a tightly-fitting plug, and nullifies your efforts. Your bowels, as a consequence, move less frequently and only after an abnormal quantity of fecal matter has been packed above the plug, or when that abnormal mass of new fecal matter initiates an extra powerful peristaltic wave in your whole alimentary tract.

But that abnormal mass also stretches your adjoining lower bowel, and so your adjoining lower bowel requires an even larger mass to dislodge the next fecal plug that forms in it. That delays your bowel movements still more, and the ever-increasing size of the fecal mass dislodges the body organs around it and compresses your prostate, bladder and rectum, and thereby obstructs still more the pathway of your stools. It also stretches and tenses the nerves of that area of your body, leaving you suffering from an infuriating itching between your buttocks (anal pruritis). By now your daily ordeals have become insufferable, and usually culminate in a frustrated failure that produces a full, throbbing sensation in your rectum and subconsciously fixes in your mind, reflexly, the pattern of failure and frustration in everything you attempt during the day. You are then far from being the man you could otherwise be.

How to Avoid Constipation

To circumvent that plagued condition, avoid constipating foods as much as possible and eat more raw fruits and fresh vegetables daily. But also get up from your desk every 50 minutes, if you possibly can, and walk around for a few minutes. (It will rest your eyes, too.)

When you are at the stool, use the Yogi Bench position and let *gravity help you* evacuate regularly and healthfully. This is accomplished by using the Yogi Bench (described in Chapter 7)

as a platform for your feet, so as to bring your knees up to a
sharper angle than the usual 90-degree angle that is assumed
when you are seated at the toilet. Sitting in a posture as on a
dining room or kitchen chair while at stool, does not utilize the
force of gravity sufficiently to aid in the evacuation process. A
Yogi assumes a practically squatty position, which brings the
knees up to a more elevated position, which is most productive
of a healthful evacuation of the bowels, and uses the right angle
of pull of the muscles for defecation. The Western conventional
method of being seated at stool, legs forming a 90 degree angle,
uses the muscles of defecation wrongly for the most healthful
results in combating constipation.

Case histories

How Vice-President Ryan Toned Up His Flabby Myotomic Muscles for Great Results

Ryan was the vice-president of a manufacturing company
dwindling fast. If the trend continued for another two years, the
company would go bankrupt. Ryan spent practically all his time
trying to find ways to turn the tide, but his thinking ended in
discouragement and despair. He tired easily at his desk and was
plagued with an insidious, nagging, tight feeling in his back that
harrassed him without letup. Matters reached the point where,
instead of concentrating clearly on the company's difficulties,
he seemed to spend as much time dreading that insidious, nagging, tight feeling in his back. At times, too, his back seemed to
throb with hot and cold sensations that were difficult to pinpoint.
Even when he lay down and tried to rest, his back throbbed. He
wished that someone would pound his back with a sledgehammer
and smash that feeling out of it. His humor had fled, and a frown
had gloomed his brow.

Ryan called on me, and I saw that he was plagued with one
of the typical, subchronic physical handicaps of the executive
and professional man—flabby myotomic muscles. I advised him to
tone them up with Yogatone, and he took my advice to heart.
Before long, his whole body and mind underwent a miraculous
change. No longer did his back feel so tired or tight in different
places, with hot and cold sensations throbbing mysteriously all
over it.

The feeling that he was so much like his old self so soon threw Ryan out of his lethargy, even though his myotomic muscles were still not fully toned up. He started thinking with a new intensity, and could hardly believe it when, as if out of the blue, one small idea followed another, and built up into one big idea with which his company could dispense with several specific, non-paying items, and take in *less* total revenue, *but yet add* nearly 25 percent to its earnings. That portentous discovery led to another, and in the amazingly brief period of two days, Ryan had worked out thoroughly a practical and realistic program to save his company from threatening bankruptcy. With Yogatone, vice-president Ryan had partly toned up his flabby myotomic muscles and had felt so differently that he had gone ahead and tackled and solved his company's fearful problem.

How Maxwell, an Accountant, Overcame His Middle Back Pain and Regained the Necessary Astuteness and Keeness of Mind

Maxwell's accounting business had mushroomed in the last few years, and his customers were highly pleased with his work. But, recently, he had made two serious errors in different accounts, and the customers were highly displeased. Maxwell was displeased with himself, too, for he felt that he had not given his best. Not that he didn't try, but he seemed to be plagued with occasional, burdensome, nagging aches and pains in the middle of his back. Nothing was found seriously wrong with his back at diagnosis, but he was advised to work fewer hours a day and give his back a chance to free itself for a while from the strains of long desk posture. But Maxwell would not. His clients depended on him, he insisted, and he could not afford to disappoint them. And so, he disregarded his physician's advice and continued doing what he was, but also continued making more, even if minor, mistakes in his work.

Since there was nothing seriously wrong with his back otherwise, I advised him to do the ergo-cross and tone up the necessary muscles of his middle back to overcome the subchronic pain. Maxwell started doing it that very day. To his astonishment, he felt the simple movement seize his drooping shoulders and hoist them up. After doing it for several days Maxwell was already experiencing, for part of the time he worked, the enjoyable bracing sensation the ergo-cross gave his shoulders, as well as its delightful squeezing out of the nagging sensitivity from his middle back. He started relishing his work again and making fewer needless mistakes. In less than a week Maxwell regained the necessary astuteness and keenness of mind that he had been steadily loosing, and felt once more like the man he used to be.

How Leslie, a Lawyer, Won His Difficult Corporation Case by Freeing His Neck from the Daily "Crippling" Feeling that Afflicted It

Leslie was a 45-year-old corporation lawyer and had done well. Now he had his biggest case, but he couldn't seem to think clearly anymore. His optimism was gone, his calm thinking was routed, and he was detesting everything about law and wishing that he had become a grocery clerk, instead. His doctor found him in good health, but occasionally Leslie experienced the beginning of a headache and a strange, creeping sensation all over his head and scalp, and even over his neck, arms, shoulders and chest. At other times, he even felt slightly giddy. Perhaps he needed a change, he felt. Yet, he could not give up the case, his biggest one to date.

Leslie held his neck in an unnatural swan-like curve, and so I advised him to do The Sitting Duck. It worked like magic on him; for, less than two minutes after doing it, his mind seemed clearer to him than it had ever been! (That, of course, was the psychological impact upon him, due to the sudden flushing of blood into his mind and to his suddenly feeling temporarily better. But it convinced him that it worked, and his enthusiasm returned in full, even long before his condition was ameliorated.) Leslie rushed back to his office and back into the case. He continued doing The Sitting Duck twice a day, no more, as I had advised him to. He was so full of "brain energy" after that, as he termed it, that he defended the corporation with remarkable ability and made a big name for himself.

Summary of the steps for using Yoga for the executive and professional man

In order to apply Yoga for the executive and professional man, you have to counteract, with Yogatone, the physical and physiological discomforts on your body caused by the four horsemen of the mastabah, and reflexly, their ill effects on *your clear thinking.* You do so by:

1. Toning up your flabby myotomic muscles.
2. Toning up, with the ergo-cross, the necessary muscles to overcome your subchronic middle back pain.
3. Opening wider the vertebral openings of your neck.
4. Relieving your constipation (even if it is unsuspected) with the Yogi Bench.

The determined, invisible hands that incessantly pull your body downwards and threaten to ruin your progress as an executive or professional man will be held in abeyance, and your mind will think again with a clarity you forgot was available!

The Yoga Secrets for Staying Younger Longer

14

The Yogis have baffled the Western world with their seemingly ageless bodies. It is not uncommon for them to live 100 years, and a startling number of them live considerably beyond that, or up to 150, 200 or more. Although the Western world refuses to believe it, there are even cases of Yogis who are declared to live up to 450. No matter how long most of them live, too, their bodies age comparatively little. These well-guarded Yoga secrets have now been carefully studied and scientifically refined for *your own use* safely in the Western world, to enable you to remain younger longer, without subjecting yourself to their awesome disciplines. The case histories prove how effective they can be for you.

How inborn power to stay young much longer is wasted

The four horsemen of the mastabah reduce your natural, inborn power to stay young longer by:

1. Hastening the aging of your tissues and organs with old-age posture.
2. Helping your arteries lose their elasticity long before they should.
3. Upsetting your sympathetic-parasympathetic nervous system balance, which maintains your physiological normalcy.

4. Increasing your possibilities of strain hernia.
5. Increasing the load on your heart.
6. Helping your tissues dry up prematurely.
7. Hastening wrinkles, stomach trouble, etc.

You will now be shown how these unwanted changes are brought about in you and reduce your natural, inborn powers to stay young much longer, and the refined, scientifically-perfected Yoga secrets for counteracting them and achieving the utmost benefits from them in your life, as swiftly as possible.

How the four horsemen hasten and multiply their deforming of your body into the crippling old-age posture that finishes your youth

Dr. Palmer found that, from birth to the age of 70, the center of gravity in the human body descends gradually from the point in your spine at the level of the bottom of your shoulder blades (*Figure 74*) to a point just below the beginning of your hips

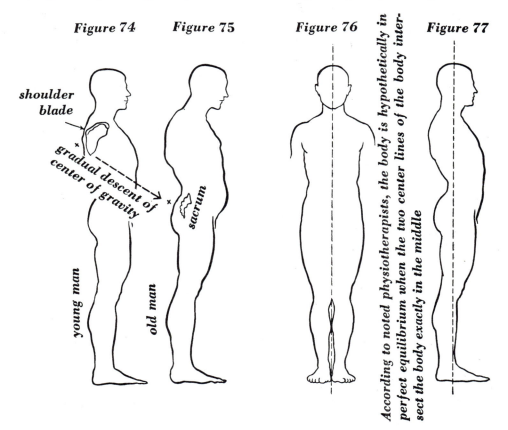

Figure 74   Figure 75   Figure 76   Figure 77

shoulder blade

gradual descent of center of gravity

sacrum

young man

old man

According to noted physiotherapists, the body is hypothetically in perfect equilibrium when the two center lines of the body intersect the body exactly in the middle

(*Figure 75*). The center of gravity is the point in your body where your body weight is perfectly balanced, or its weight evenly distributed (*Figures 76, 77*). When your center of gravity descends, as it does with age, it indicates that your torso has shortened, and that you have acquired wrong-back curves and faulty posture. (The Yoga secrets are especially based on retaining the center of gravity of the body *at least* at the height it was when the body was young and its legs had attained their full length . . . that is, before its back had shortened much, its wrong-back curves formed deeply, or its faulty posture developed significantly.)

To stave off old age posture, then, you have to prevent the center of gravity in your body from falling. Otherwise, you acquire old age posture over the years, and it lowers your center of gravity still more, thins your spinal disks prematurely, and brings on arthritis and other degenerative diseases of the spine which seriously reduce your natural, inborn power to stay young. "Old age," said a renowned orthopedist, "is the net result of bad habits." He could have added, "And a significant number of those bad habits are due to the helpless struggle waged between the unprepared body and the relentless body traumas of gravity, faulty posture, weight-bearing and ground resistance."

While it is usual for chronic ailments and disabilities to make their appearance with advancing age, that is not necessarily so. While aging is a normal physiological process, and even while we cannot prevent it, we *can* prevent or *delay* much of its accompanying discomfort and disability.

A number of structural changes in the body invariably accompany aging. One of the most obvious is the change in body carriage. The head bends forward, like a duck about to peck at the ground. The back bows, and the vertebral rib joints stiffen. The abdominal muscles weaken and sag, and the abdominal organs protrude. The hips are drawn in, the normal curve of the lower back is increasingly flattened. The knees are slightly bent, and the arches of the feet give. The gait resembles that of a dejected beggar.

A man's nervous system degenerates and slows its speed of transmitting messages from his body to his brain, and of commands from his brain to his body, causing a slowing down of his reflexes. In his brain there is a certain amount of reversal of the normal order of growth and development of its cells (involution), due to the reduced blood circulation and hardening of the arteries in it. In his body, tremors result from the degeneration of his brain and nervous system.

Many other conditions affect the skeleton in old age, and sometimes they are very crippling and deforming. One of them, whose incidence is universally increasing, is osteoporosis (an increasing porosity and softening of the bone) of the spine. Osteoporosis is the chief cause of the fractures of the brittle bones of the aged. The ligaments have lost their elasticity, and the spinal disks have thinned, and so the spine bows gradually, along the years, into old age posture (senile kyphosis). Add to it the effects of the lowered heart and slumping rib-box, and this—the old age posture—can result in serious disability. Obviously, your youth is then finished.

How to prolong youthful middle-age and avoid the crippling, youth-diminishing old age posture

With a diet rich in calcium, and with Yogametric exercises to encourage more lifelong bone growth, much of the osteoporosis of advancing years can be sternly combated. By keeping your glandular tissues supplied with as much nutritive blood as possible, the remaining cause of osteoporosis (the glandular cause) can also be minimized. With correct posture and toned up myotomic and other back muscles, serious wrong-back curves can be prevented. And, even when serious deformity has already resulted, as Lewin pointed out before, the most serious symptoms can be relieved with the use of special positions and exercises by the therapist to improve body mechanics. The Yogis were right in claiming that they *did* prolong their youthful middle-age and *did* avoid the crippling, youth-finishing old age posture.

The Yoga secret to prevent the onset of youth-finishing old age posture

The Yoga secret to prevent the onset of youth-finishing old age posture is the Yogametric simple movement, The Youth Look Insurer, described as follows:

The Youth Look Insurer

The position to assume

1. Stand with your back against the free edge of an opened door. (Closet door should do.)
2. Place tips of fingers of each hand on its corresponding half of the top edge of the door. If you are too short, stand on a chair, solid box or secure stool
3. Your elbows will be bent and pointing outwards.

How to do this simple movement

4. Pull down hard with the tips of your fingers. At the same time
5. Draw your elbows backwards.
6. Your shoulders will be drawn inwards and upwards, thus stretching the ligaments of your shoulder girdle and shoulder blades, and broadening your shoulders.
7. Your biceps will be contracted tightly.
8. Your trapezius will be contracted tightly.
9. Your waist will be stretched.
10. Your spine will be stretched.

This simple movement develops:

1. Trapezius. (Thus holds up shoulders.)
2. Posterior deltoids. (Thus holds back shoulders.)
3. Both heads of biceps. (Gives arms the sought-after peak. They hold up the arms.)
4. Undersides of forearms. (Also hold up the arms.)
5. Broadens the shoulders. (Prevents old age shoulder narrowing.)
6. Thins the waist. (Prevents old age waist thickening.)
7. Stretches spine. (Prevents old age wrong-back curving, such as senile kyphosis.) This is another unbelievably effective, yet very simple movement.

Frequency

3–4 times a day.

How the loss of elasticity of your larger arteries and the frequent accompanying narrowing of your smaller arteries age you fast

The elasticity of your arteries is the power of the muscles in their walls to recoil when your arteries are stretched wide by the blood flowing through them during the intervals between your heart beats. That elasticity enables your arteries to maintain your diastolic blood pressure. Your diastolic blood pressure is the lower of the two readings recorded when your blood pressure is taken. It reveals the pressure of the blood flowing through your arteries when their walls are *stretched out wide* by the blood filling them, and your heart is therefore momentarily pumping *no* blood into them.

Your systolic blood pressure, in contrast, is the one which you are regularly given at diagnosis. It reveals the pressure of the blood flowing through your arteries when their walls *have narrowed fully*, and your heart is again pumping blood into them, to fill them. If your arteries were rigid, instead, and could *not* be widened or narrowed, your arteries could then *not* narrow again, once they were widened, and squeeze the blood in them onwards.

But since your arteries *do* possess muscles in their walls which *do* recoil when stretched out wide and which, consequently, narrow the arteries once more, the blood which your heart pumps into your arteries is forced onwards steadily, in a continuous stream, even during the intervals between your heart beats, during which your heart is momentarily pumping *no* blood into your arteries. Any hardening (that is, any *loss* of elasticity) of the walls of your arteries, then (provided that all other contributing factors remain unchanged), tends to *lower* your diastolic blood pressure because it tends to *weaken* the power of recoil of the muscles of your arterial walls.

The muscles of your larger arteries, though, harden and stretch less and less with the years. For that reason, their power of recoil against the blood being pumped into your larger arteries weakens as you get older, and your blood pressure falls. The hardening of the muscles of your larger arteries, however, is frequently accompanied by a narrowing of your *smaller* arteries, and that, in turn, *raises* your blood pressure and offsets any fall in it resulting from the hardening of your larger arteries. That's why in order to remain young longer, you must try to prevent your larger arteries from hardening (losing their elasticity), and your smaller arteries from narrowing (and raising your blood pressure).

How to help prevent your larger arteries from hardening and losing their elasticity

Your larger arteries are the main ones concerned with hardening, because their muscles compose about half the thickness of their walls. Like all other muscles, those of your arteries degenerate comparatively early when not regularly bathed with enough nutrition-carrying blood. That occurs when the nerves controlling their blood supply are squeezed by narrowed vertebral openings, or when you flood your arteries repeatedly with an over-abundance of polysaturated fats, or when you don't exercise sufficiently and regularly enough to enable your arteries to dislodge the accumulated waste products from their inner surfaces faster, but instead allow their unexercised muscle fibers to degenerate irreversibly into fatty tissue. Exercise retains the elasticity of your arterial walls by forcing them to stretch widely and contract narrowly, in order to help your pumping heart rush more blood to your skeletal muscles, and those movements in themselves develop the muscles of your arteries. The violent stretching and contracting of the arterial muscles during exercise, too, discourage fat from depositing in them, because more calories are then burned up in them, and the fat being brought to them is therefore used up faster. The repetitious widening and narrowing of the arteries which takes place during exercise, also, wears off or throws off the fat that tries to deposit on them. Reducing your consumption of fatty foods is important because it lessens the amount of exercise you need for "shaking" the accumulating fat off your arterial walls.

How your smaller arteries narrow prematurely, raise your blood pressure, and shorten your youth and your life significantly

Exercise and reduced fat intake, for the same reasons described above, help prevent your smaller arteries from narrowing prematurely. But there is *another important cause* for their narrowing prematurely—a cause that has baffled medical science for centuries. It is clinically called *essential (or benign) hypertension*.

Although the actual cause of essential hypertension is unknown, the nervous system, the kidneys, liver, pancreas and adrenal glands are suspect to blame. The nervous system is blamed for causing it through a hypersensitivity of the sympathetics (the nerves that widen or narrow the arteries, and thereby control the blood circulation), and the resulting overintensification of their commands to the muscles of the arteries to relax or recoil.

The kidney, though, is also to blame, for it directly causes the blood pressure to rise by secreting into the bloodstream a substance, renin. And *that is what* has perplexed the scientific world so long. *Why does the kidney secrete renin into the body and cause hypertension?*

Amazing to state, it is rather simply explained by the principles of Yoga. As your body proceeds in regularly combating the relentless four horsemen, your subconscious mind commands your sympathetics to help it meet the emergency. Your sympathetics do so by widening the smaller arteries of your muscles, in order to supply them with more nutritive blood to enable them to resist those four enemies better. Simultaneously, your sympathetics *narrow* the smaller arteries of your visceral organs (like those of your kidney, liver, pancreas and adrenal glands), in order to supply them with *less* nutritive blood and let your muscles have more of it instead. Your kidneys, liver, pancreas and adrenal glands, though, are vital organs of the utmost importance in your body, and so these instinctively, after suffering from blood starvation long enough, try to draw more nutritive blood *back into them* from your monopolizing muscles, in order to function again normally.

In order to prevent your arteries from narrowing prematurely, then, you have to prevent your sympathetic nervous system from predominating over your parasympathetics and thereby from chronically contracting the muscles of the walls of the smaller arteries of your skeletal muscles. You achieve this by restoring and maintaining sympathetic-parasympathetic nervous system balance.

NOTE: High blood pressure not only causes wear-and-tear injury of the arterial wall through the increased friction of the blood flow against it, but also provides the "percolation pressure" necessary to imbed the large lipid (fat) molecules being carried in the blood (from eating fatty foods), into the cells lining the inner wall of the artery. Josué produced arterial degeneration in rabbits by daily injections of adrenalin. The adrenalin, which acts as though overstimulating the sympathetics, caused the blood pressure of the rabbits to rise, and then the increased friction of the blood provided the "percolation pressure" necessary to imbed the fat molecules being carried in the blood of the rabbits, into the inner walls of the arteries of the rabbits and form atheromatous plaques: or the dreaded, life-shortening arterial wall deposits which form when the cholesterol level of the blood rises, and which causes blood clots. This is another important reason why you *have* to restore sympathetic-parasympathetic balance in you, if you wish to stay young longer.

How to regain natural, inborn sympathetic-parasympathetic nervous system balance by recharging your endocrine glands

The body traumas of the horsemen of the mastabah, together with poor psychological habits, produce imbalance between your sympathetics (your fighting nerves) and your parasympathetics (your loving nerves). They do so by compelling your body to waste excessive energy in trying to keep the two of them balanced to sustain you in normal health in the "unnatural" two-footed position. The resulting imbalance predisposes you towards a sympathetic nervous system predominance in your body, such as to excessive tone of the nerves carrying messages from your body to your brain to prepare you swiftly to meet emergencies; to excessive tone of the nerves delivering commands from your brain to your body to meet the emergency; to undue alertness of your conscious and subconscious minds to any sudden physiological imbalance like the unexpected demands of a "nervous" heart, of unstable blood pressure, as well as of the demands on you caused by fear, anger, and so forth. When you lie down and rest you reduce that sympathetic nervous system predominance considerably. Otherwise, the two-legged position keeps you hypersympathetic in tone, and leaves your parasympathetics perpetually striving to restore the lost equilibrium between the two of them. This equilibrium is maintained only when the sensitivity of one of them equals that of the other. Maintaining the balance between these two nervous systems, in fact, is the basic secret of "perpetual youth." Balancing and keeping them balanced causes a "rebirth" of the degenerated endocrine glands, especially of the thyroid and adrenal. In the most spectacular Yogi cases, such an achievement is followed by the growth of a new head of hair with youthful pigment, a new set of teeth, renewed sex potency, loss of hardness of the arteries as the fatty deposits melt out of their muscles and away from their walls, and the blooming forth of new, young skin which makes the Yogi look like 35 at 172. Balance these two nervous systems in you by "rejuvenating" your thyroid and adrenal glands. Do it exactly as the Yogi does it.

The Yoga secret for rejuvenating the thyroid gland

One thyroid gland lies on each side of your windpipe, at the base of your throat. Your thyroid is important for keeping you young much longer than otherwise because its chief function is to increase the different unions with oxygen that take place in your body. On account of that, it stimulates your growth and metabolic processes generally, and therefore has a marked influence upon your bone development, sexual phenomena, blood sugar, blood pressure, water balance, blood manufacture, heart, liver, and sympathetic nerves and adrenal glands. It also influences your ability to fight off disease, and meet danger and emergency. For a long time the Yogi knew that the thyroid gland region of his body significantly affected the rest of it, and particularly when his rejuvenation was concerned. Consequently, he perfected specific simple movements to stimulate this first half of his process of rejuvenation.

Your thyroid gland can be affected by stimulating the muscles of your shoulder, and also the sympathetic ganglia in your upper back. The simple Yogametric movement for it is The Bent-Arm Backward Drive, described as follows.

THE BENT-ARM BACKWARD DRIVE

The position to assume

1. Sit on a chair.
2. Set your elbows three-fourths upwards from the ground. (135 degree angle above the ground.)
3. Flex your forearms.
4. Clench your fists, and
5. Turn thumb-halves backwards.

How to do this simple movement

6. Inhale and draw your arms backwards and downwards hard, so that they
7. Contract stiffly at about 45 degree angles from the ground.

Try to make your arms meet in back. Of course you can't. Trying to do so, though, contracts your middle upper back muscles to the full.

What this simple movement does for you:

It develops your

1. Trapezius (fourth section).
2. Rhomboids.
3. Posterior deltoid.

Contracting these muscles stimulates the sympathetic ganglia in your upper back, and your thyroid glands. The attachments of your trapezius and rhomboids include the first 4 vertebrae of your upper back, and these control your upper sympathetic ganglia. These, in turn, control the blood supply to your thyroid.

Frequency

2–4 times a day; 3–5 times a week.

The Yoga secret for rejuvenating the adrenal gland

One adrenal gland lies immediately above each kidney. Your adrenal gland is important for keeping you young because its outer portion has many functions. It furnishes, for one thing, the energizing substances of your body. It influences your growth, metabolism and sexual development. It increases your energy, protects you against infections, and acts in concert with adrenalin to subdue your increased susceptibility to infection when you suffer a second attack of the same infectious malady. It also relieves you from the effects of allergies.

When your adrenal gland is deficient, your body salts and sugars decrease, and your blood turns more acid than normal. At the same time, your potassium ions, your tissue wastes and cholesterol *increase*, robbing you of your youth and shortening your life. For a long time, too, the Yogi knew that the adrenal gland region of his body significantly affected the rest of it, and particularly when his rejuvenation was concerned. Consequently, he perfected a specific simple movement to stimulate this second half of his process of rejuvenation. That simple movement is The Downward Eagle Spread.

THE DOWNWARD EAGLE SPREAD

The position to assume
1. Stand with feet hip-width (8 inches apart).
2. Hold a rolled newspaper in back of you.
3. Hands close together.
4. Palms facing forwards.
5. Back straight.
6. Draw shoulders down low.
7. Inhale and expand your chest.

How to do this simple movement
1. Exhale,
2. Arch your back, and
3. Draw hands backwards and upwards *far enough* . . . tightening your lower middle back muscles hard. Keep shoulders LOW.
4. Relax, exhale and repeat.

What this simple movement does for you:

It develops speedily, bulging, well-defined, lower middle back muscles; your

1. Trapezius (fourth section).
2. Rhomboids.
3. Posterior deltoid.
4. Sacrospinalis.

Contracting these muscles stimulates the sympathetic ganglia in your middle lower back, and your adrenal glands. The attachments of your rhomboids and trapezius and sacrospinalis include the fifth to ninth vertebrae of your back (or those of your lower middle back), and these control those sympathetic ganglia. These sympathetics, in turn, control the blood supply to your adrenal glands.

5. Triceps (inner).
6. Forearms (underside).

Frequency

2–4 times a day; 3–5 times a week.

It is impossible to overpraise the results of the Upward and Downward Eagle Spreads on the impressive knotty contouring of your whole back.

How to minimize the possibilities of strain hernia by keeping your abdominal wall sufficiently toned with the Yogametric abdominal massager

There are many kinds of hernia. The congenital (inherited) variety, due to imperfections of the abdominal wall or to any other reason, usually require surgery. Everybody, though, because of the four horsemen, is subject to strain hernia, no matter how perfectly constructed his abdominal wall may be, when he lifts a weight or exerts a force with his body strenuous enough to push the contents of his abdominal cavity so forcibly against his abdominal muscles that they may bulge through it in a tight, excruciatingly painful, little ball of flesh. If you stop the exertion at once and press hard upon the painful spot with your hand, you can press the little ball of flesh back. But if your abdominal muscles lack sufficient tone, you might find yourself having a true hernia.

Since it can happen to anybody, because of the relentless downpull of gravity, your only recourse is to minimize the possibilities of its occurrence and try to avoid becoming the victim of a chronic, recurrent hernia. The Yogis, who have to strain their bodies regularly in their rugged existence, prepare themselves against strain hernia by keeping their abdominal walls always sufficiently toned. The Yogametric abdominal massager is their simple movement for it. Its method is described as follows:

THE YOGAMETRIC ABDOMINAL MASSAGER

The position to assume

1. Lie flat on your bed, or on a softened floor. Do not lie on the hard, bare floor.
2. Lie on your back.
3. Stretch arms out directly in back of your head.

How to do this simple movement

4. Inhale deeply.
5. Curl your toes toward your head.

6. Now, gather your strength and *exhale* as you
7. Raise your arms and legs *at the same time.*
8. Raise your legs no higher than 45 degrees from the ground.
9. Raise your body as you bring your arms forward and downward, as if trying to touch your toes with your fingers.
10. Relax and repeat.

This simple movement develops:

All the muscles of your abdomen: your rectus abdominis, and the external and internal obliques. Therefore, it protects unsurpassably against hernia.

Frequency

3 times a day. 5 days a week.

This is perhaps the greatest abdominal exercise of all. It does miracles for your waistline, for your liver, stomach, circulation and heart. Make it a daily "must" for the rest of your life.

How to keep your heart younger by lessening its load

Like the Yogi, you can keep your heart younger by lessening its load. You lessen its load by increasing the superior mechanical ability of your muscles to replenish their energy when fatigued. Through the ability of your muscles to contract *even when* deprived of oxygen, and to replenish their stores of energy *even while* regaining their oxygen loss, they are able to perform, for short periods, an amount of work which they could NOT perform if they were, like the motor engine, dependent *entirely* upon a *contemporaneous* oxygen supply. This unusual ability of your muscles is an unsurpassed youth preserver, for it saves your heart a lot of work.

Since you cannot rest immediately after every time you exert yourself, this unsurpassed ability of your muscles soon loses its effectiveness after exertion, and the lactic acid accumulates in your muscles. This leads to a feeling of fatigue which you regularly ignore and, on account of that, risk overstraining your muscles. You also risk overstraining your heart, not only for that same reason, but also because the lactic acid itself depletes the protein reserves of your muscles and weakens their tissues, including that of your heart muscle. The Yogi meets this emergency and, consequently, lessens the load on his heart and keeps it younger, with the Breathe-Third-Breathe to the Breathe-Full-Breathe.

Yoga secret for keeping the heart younger after exertion

The Breathe-Third-Breathe, to the Breathe-Full-Breathe, is the phenominal Yoga secret for lessening the load on the heart during fatiguing exertion, and thereby for keeping it younger much longer. It is simple to do:

As you warm up during physical exertion, begin to feel tired and breathe more deeply, your heart will pump stronger, and therefore work harder to drive more oxygen into your oxygen-begging muscles. Instead of continuing to breathe deeper and deeper, though, until you are overcome with fatigue, do the following:

1. Breathe out only *one-third* of your deep breathing breath, and then
2. Quickly fill your lungs again with air. Oxygen is rushed faster to your lungs then than if you waited until your *whole* deep breathing breath was exhaled before you inhaled again.
3. Repeat that procedure several times, as you continue with the exertion.
4. Then go on deep breathing as usual.
5. When you are feeling noticeably tired again and are breathing too deeply, repeat the procedure (from Nos. 1 to 4).

That's all there is to it.

You will find that the Breathe-Third-Breathe, to the Breathe-Full-Breathe, revives you astoundingly. It does so by supplying your muscles with *decidedly more oxygen* than they would receive from your regular deep breathing during the exertion. Your muscles, then, demand *less* oxygen for a while afterwards than they would otherwise. Your heart will, as a result, be called upon to pump *less hard* for a while than it would pump otherwise and would, for that reason, be practically "resting" during that interval. By repeating the Breathe-Third-Breathe, to the Breathe-Full-Breathe, several times during the exertion, you will succeed in "resting" your heart regularly during the effort.

Practice this simple, but truly amazing, Yoga secret, a few times, in order to do it right, and be ready to use it the next time you exert yourself fatiguingly, such as when you jog. Not only will it increase your endurance amazingly, but it also will lessen the load from your heart and keep it younger decidedly longer.

How to keep your tissues from drying up sooner than they should and making you look old prematurely

A long time ago, the Yogis observed that those who lived near the Indian Desert looked much older for their years than those who lived near the coast or in other damp, watery regions, mainly because their skin wrinkled markedly sooner and deeper. Many who lived in the more rainy, cloudy regions, indeed, retained their youthful appearances until advanced age. The Yogis therefor concluded, and apparently rightly so, that in order to stay young looking, a person had to imbibe enough water daily to to prevent his tissues from drying up prematurely. They noticed that the same phenomenon occurred with fruit on trees. On the very same tree, the fruit that faced the sun *less* directly dried up far less and far slower than the fruit that faced the sun *more* directly. Since, to the Yogi, the outside of the fruit represented what happened to the inside of it, he concluded that, if he did inside him what kept the skin outside him young, it would keep the organs inside him young, too.

The solution is simple. Drink adequate amounts of youth-preserving (both inside and outside) water daily.

Drink one and a half glasses of warm water immediately upon arising.

Drink about one and a half glasses *twice* between breakfast and lunch, an hour apart from each other.

Drink the same quantity between lunch and supper.

Total: Eight glasses.

This is one of the most important habitual self-rejuvenating measures of the Yogi. *Do not* count liquids taken at meal time. Those are part of your regular meals, whether they be skimmed milk, fruit juices or even water. (Tea, coffee, and other stimulants do not count either. Indeed, they should be avoided altogether if you really want to stay young much longer.)

Case histories

How Executive Wayne, at 53, Rejuvenated Himself with Yogametrics

Wayne had been with the same company for 30 years and had risen to the top executive post in his department.

Then his world caved in on him. His company merged with another, and Wayne was suddenly a supernumerary. He dragged himself out of the company doors for the last time, completely stunned.

He took a week to recuperate, then started looking for another position, satisfied that his long years with the one company would be a decided advantage to him. To his bewilderment, he was rejected by company after company!

For two whole years Wayne frantically called on one employment bureau after another and answered every want-ad that held out the faintest possibility for him. But he got no work.

Wayne confided his predicament to me. Although he was naturally about 5′ 10″, Wayne measured only about 5′ 7½″, and looked about 5′ 6″. His legs seemed to extend about three-fourths up his full height because his torso had shrunk so much. And his head seemed to be trying to bend down and touch his body, while his back had looped backwards in a deep curve. His deformed torso, in fact, had grown so ungracefully short and thick from front to back that it suggested a buffalo's. When he sat down, it humped over still more. No one who did not know him well would accept him readily for an energetic, determined man with an alert mind. His face, too, was unusually dry and drawn and, with his truncated torso, added another 15 years to his apparent age. Wayne confessed to me, too, that he suffered occasionally from vague pains in his back and that he constantly felt as if a ponderous mass was pressing down on his back and exhausting it.

Since, upon diagnosis, he was found to be normal enough otherwise, I put him on a Yoga self-rejuvenating program. I had him drink ten glasses of water a day, and do the Youth Look Insurer to lessen considerably his old age posture and reduce its crippling effects. When I saw him again, three months later, he had gained about four pounds of fluid weight and his face had lost its dehydrated look and had acquired a suggestion of a younger freshness. His torso, best of all, was noticeably more erect; the distance between his chin and his waist had lengthened and suggested more that of a decidedly younger man. His vague, occasional nagging pains had practically vanished. Observing his own unbelievable change had exhilarated Wayne, and he had cast off the defeated, pessimistic attitude that had clouded his face from the day he had shockingly lost his job.

Once again he burst with enthusiasm and called once more on prospective employers.

This time he landed a good position, although he was now 57! With his energy, determination and keen thinking he revamped the tottering company. In less than a year and a half, he had put it in the black and had been granted a small raise, with promises of much better ones as the company prospered. Wayne was convinced that it would. With Yogametrics, Wayne had rejuvenated himself at 57 and come back and made good again in life.

How a 62-Year-Old Dentist, Remade Himself with Yogametrics after Recuperating from a Heart Attack

Dr. Quinn (not his real name) was a hard-working, enthusiastic, highly-respected dentist. He had been practicing for nearly 40 years, and looked forward to retiring soon.

Instead, he suffered a heart attack. As he lay in the hospital, with his chest so painful that he could hardly breathe, Dr. Quinn was too despondent for words. For years his doctor had warned him of that possibility and had sternly ordered him to smoke less, eat fewer cholesterol depositing foods, reduce tremendously his sizable intake of coffee, and engage in regular exercise, even after he had been standing for hours all day at his chair. But Dr. Quinn had ignored the orders and had continued practicing dentistry in order to retire and enjoy life.

I knew Dr. Quinn well. I managed to convince him, once he left the hospital, that his doctor was right. So he reduced his fatty foods to a minimum and jogged, doing the Breathe-Third-Breathe, to the Breathe-Full-Breathe, to take some of the load off his heart. His heart grew steadily stronger, and so he jogged further and further regularly and even bragged about it. Finally, he added Yogametrics to stimulate his thyroid and adrenal glands, and started looking younger, too! He found, besides, that his long daily practice was exhausting him less and less! His dreams of a wonderful retirement returned, for he was feeling as strong and young as he had at 35, and was now looking more as he did at 45! With Yogametrics, 62-year-old Dr. Quinn remade himself after recuperating from a heart attack.

Summary of the steps for using Yoga for staying young much longer

In order to apply the well-guarded Yoga secrets for staying young much longer, you have to counteract the youth-robbing devastations of your body effected by the relentless horsemen of the mastabah. You do so by Yoga wisdom in:

1. Prolonging youthful middle-age and avoiding the crippling, youth-finishing, old age posture.
2. Helping prevent your larger arteries from hardening prematurely and losing their elasticity.
3. Helping prevent your smaller arteries from narrowing prematurely and raising your blood pressure.
4. Regaining natural, inborn sympathetic-parasympathetic nervous system balance by recharging your endocrine glands.
5. Minimizing the possibilities of strain hernia.
6. Keeping your heart younger by lessening its load.
7. Keeping your tissues from drying up prematurely (and thereby making you look old prematurely).

The Yota-Yoga —the Yoga Secret

15

Now that you have re-widened your narrowed vertebral openings significantly and have regained much of your lost, natural, inborn powers, *you have to accustom your subconscious mind to accept that change in you as a fact,* and therefore to put those powers of yours into use *any time you wish.* To guarantee that it will do so, you have to trigger your reluctant subconscious mind *to accept those regained powers in you as actual facts* EVERY TIME, and at the VERY TIME, that you want to use any of them. The well-guarded Yoga secret for triggering your subconscious mind into doing that is the Yota-Yoga.

Here is how to do the Yota-Yoga.

A. First of all, develop super-sympathetic nervous system control. In order to do so,

1. Sit comfortably in a chair and place your opened palms together before you, as in the position of prayer.
2. Push together, with equal strength, one palm against the other.
3. When you get too strong for that, place both your palms and your forearms together at the same time, and press the whole lengths of your hands and forearms harder and harder together.

4. When you think you can press them together no harder, press them still harder together. To do so, think of something that makes you boiling mad, and pour that anger into your pressing hands and forearms.
5. Do Nos. 1 to 4 for about two weeks, two or three times a day when your stomach is empty.

B. After two weeks your muscles will be strong enough to allow you to develop *de-conscious control.* To do so,

6. Repeat Nos. 1 to 5. But now forget completely that you are pressing with your hands and forearms, and just press all the harder.
7. Let no caution or inhibition lessen your pressing power in the least.
8. Your brain will automatically secrete the unknown right chemical substance necessary to relax both your conscious and subconscious minds. (The brain secretes an ever-growing list of unknown chemical substances which control the functions of the body.)
9. Relax the contraction after two or three seconds, and and then repeat Nos. 6 to 8.

That is how the champion athlete breaks records. He applies more and more power to his efforts, but with *no emotion whatsoever.* The murderous punching power of winners like Jack Dempsey and Rockey Marciano, even when these gladiators seemed beaten and exhausted, attests to the untapped power of the subconscious mind. It is equally effective for mental and creative achievements, as evidenced by the confessions of great inventors and authors.

That, simply explained, is the Yota-Yoga. Use it secretly shortly before confronting anything important or meeting an emergency in your life. It will trigger in you the invincible power of your subconscious mind and enable you to apply at once, and at its maximum, any Yoga power.

In just seconds a day

You need to spend *only 49 seconds or so a day* doing the simple Yogatone and Yogametric movements of the well-guarded Yoga secrets, unless you wish to develop the Mr. America type of muscles. Don't do all the simple movements each day either, but only those that lead to your particular goal. In most cases, repeat each simple movement just once or twice—but do it *perfectly*. If you wish to develop one specific attribute, like a trim waistline or a huge biceps, repeat the particular simple movement or movements for it up to ten times, and skip some of the other simple movements for the time being.

One or two repetitions of each simple movement will tone you up and help keep you in good condition, though, because each one contracts the muscles it uses, at their right angles of pull, or at their angles of greatest contraction, and thereby tightens most of their fibers with one repetition. Those for "stretching" the muscles of your back, or any other muscles, need to be repeated only once, too, because they are designed to stretch them at their greatest length. Consequently, they don't have to be repeated, unless the muscle or ligament is unusually stiff, or when it is subjecting you to vague, undiagnosable pains.

In that way, without counting the time spent changing from one simple movement to another, you need to spend no more than a few seconds a day of actual toning or exercising with Yoga in order to reach and stay in satisfactory shape.

The new, Yoga-powered you

You have just been revealed a wealth of health; strength- and mind-sharpening Yoga secrets which are so well-guarded that never before have they been brought to light. Not only that, but they have been scientifically refined for you to enable you to profit from them as much as possible without risking the dangers of which the professionally untrained person may be unaware. Use them daily, and let them keep you mentally and physically prepared to make fast progress in anything you undertake. Turn to the simple movements again and again, and read their descriptions. These well-guarded Yoga secrets are packed with so much previously unrevealed information that you can hardly do more than grasp them with one reading. They are bursting with the voluminous, but distilled, knowledge of 133 years of research by four generations of men in my family.

With your mind and body toned up now from the simple movements of these Yoga secrets, you resume life like a different person.

With Yoga sex appeal, you meet the woman you want.

With Yoga self-mastery, you cast off your bad habits.

With Yoga power for concentration, you engross yourself in any subject, anywhere, at any time, and do expertly in it.

With Yoga for self-protection, you vanquish ominous bullies without lifting a finger.

With Yoga for energy, you are practically tireless.

With Yoga for big, powerful muscles, you may develop a Mr. America-type physique much faster than you ever dreamed of.

With Yoga for sex power, you no longer feel inadequate to the occasion.

With Yoga for popularity, you make people like you despite themselves.

With Yoga for leadership, you can stop hiding yourself, step out into the world, and be strongly supported by others.

With Yoga for the executive and professional man, you advance to the heights in your career.

With Yoga for banishing disease, you enjoy every day of your life, as well as reduce your doctor bills amazingly.

With Yoga for staying young much longer, you remain attractive to the opposite sex much longer, and are also promoted faster and more consistently. With Yoga for rolling back old age, you not only live longer and longer, but also look and feel many years younger, as you do it.

With Yoga for subconscious-mind power, you control your subconscious mind and make full use of your untapped hidden powers.

You are no longer puzzled as you were before about your body and your hidden powers. With the perfected, well-guarded Yoga secrets, you can now make your mind and body do practical "miracles" for you. Yes, you can be the Yoga-Powered You—a man with true *power knowledge*, who accomplishes what he wants to do.

Index